THE COLLECTED POEMS
of
RICHARD
CHURCH

LONDON: J. M. DENT & SONS LTD.

Made in Great Britain
by
The Temple Press · Letchworth · Herts.
First published 1948

CONTENTS

PART ONE

LYRICAL POEMS, 1942–7

PART TWO

THE DREAM AND OTHER POEMS, 1927

PART THREE

THEME WITH VARIATIONS, 1928

PART FOUR

MOOD WITHOUT MEASURE, 1928
A GROUP OF POEMS IN FREE VERSE

PART FIVE

THE GLANCE BACKWARD, 1930

PART SIX

NEWS FROM THE MOUNTAIN, 1932

PART SEVEN

TWELVE NOON, 1936

THE SOLITARY MAN, 1941

PART NINE

THE PORTRAIT OF THE ABBOT, 1926
PHILIP, 1920

PART TEN
EARLY POEMS, 1910–1926

PART ONE

LYRICAL POEMS

1942–7

The Fallow Field

GOOD to see the ploughed earth!
Here in a world of broken faith
Is something to be understood;
Man's work, Man's worth,
The labour of the share, the scope
Of our belief, our hope.

Here is something Man has made
And will remake, age after age,
Defying every tyrant's rage
With a simple thing—the spade.
Take a handful, feel it rough,
Feel it work upon your skin!
This is the elemental stuff
From whose obduracy we win
First things first, the bud, the flower,
And last, the Bread of Life.
These things are good;
These are the moments worth our strife.
Leave the tyrant to his hour:
He has never understood.

Safety in Philosophy

The wise man, sunlight dappling his hair,
Sat in the rising grass.   A million fingers
Caressed his feet, took greenhold of his chair.
His disciples spoke together; 'If he lingers,
He 'll sink knee-deep into the chlorophyl.
The running green will touch his finger-tips;
And while he meditates, the earth-tide will
Reach up, and lap with poison at his lips.'
This prophecy no sooner uttered, than
They whetted a curved hook, and chose a wrist
To venture near and save the thinking man;
And if he should refuse to move, insist!

They did not see that where he sat profound,
The mocking gods had conjured stony ground.

The Fabulous Morning

Over the tops of the elm trees
Day broke at last; the cattle stood
With the dew-mist about their knees.
Darkness still lingered in the wood.

The sleeping and the waking world
Divided, and gave place to one
Which Hellas in her sculpture told,
And poets will tell when I am gone.

The Gambler

Here is a thought come late in life,
Cutting against the grain of habit,
That I should waste no more desire
On moulding words, as a mason handles
Limestone or marble, shaping a house.

Late revolutions are the most bloody,
And I foresee in this a loud
And utterly destructive uproar,
Confusion to my mind, and sickness
To nerves already weary of strife
In one domain.   For words are kingship;
They have their fame; are made to shine
Through generation after generation
Of men whose minds are hungry for symbols
Less corruptible than graven
Stone; for words can be set singing
Like the sons of morning, if the craft be right.

Such was my discipline, a strife
Through youth, to the mature man's effort.
And now I'd turn it to account
Some other way, while in my error
Exulting, gambling late on one
Superb, yet possible result,
To let a life-time's echoes ground
In silence, for one woman's love.

4

Wartime Christmas

The bell-ropes hang unhandled
In steeple, tower, and spire.
This is the silent Christmas
Through every English shire.

He who would raise a carol
To greet his Lord and God,
Must think of rape and murder,
And the blood-soaked sod.

In silence to the Manger
We come to greet the Birth;
The Infant with His Mother,
The Saviour of the Earth.

The Three Wise Men of Asia,
The shepherds from near home,
The Star and Herald Angels—
This year they have not come.

He will not mind, the Outcast,
The Manger-born, the Child
Who to the ways of treason
Long since was reconciled.

He knows how man dissembles
The vilest shape that be
In air, on land, or under
The waters of the sea.

He knows that soon or later
This murderer will turn
In innocence and terror,
And come to Him to learn.

And not till then will Christmas,
With Shepherd's crook and Star,
Ring goodwill bells and summon
The Wise Men from afar.

Dust and Ashes

When young, I was a rival to the storm-cock.
I knew a joyfuller song than the blackbird sings
When he has cleaned his oboe-beak on wings
That but a moment since beat out a challenge
To April treachery, or frosty weather
In May.   I, too, had proud defiant things
To shout against the chill delay life brings
When youth and early hope are bud and blossom.

But Autumn is more sober.   Songs are lost
After an anxious summer seeking worms.
Blackbird and thrush and I are of a feather,
Silent now we have won what we craved most.
Is it the memory of outridden storms
That comes like frost upon the golden harvest?

The End of Drought

South-west by west they came,
The cumulus in sail,
Before each breast a burst of rain
And scattered glints of hail.

The earth looked up with dusty lips
And drank the milk of life;
The grasses touched with finger-tips,
The trees drank with delight.

Hidden far down, but hungry too,
The roots' deep fibres dared
To drink and drink until the good
Harvest was prepared.

Autumn

My heart is in September,
As with old friends departing
After the talk and harvest
Of thought and gentle deeds.

I know I shall remember
The sun so ripe in wisdom,
The voice of deep compassion,
The gathering of seeds.

The Wheel

If Time is a wheel whose measure
Runs out two thousand years,
Then the moment approaches
For someone to be born
In a world of wars and hunger,
With anarchy abroad.

The family is scattered,
The over-crowded inns
With soldiery are noisy.
For taxes and attesting
Young parents wander wide.

Maybe the wheel is slowing,
That some arterial road
In Europe or Malaya
Shall crowd itself, and stop
Either a Jew or Gentile
And force him with his bride
To shelter in a garage,
And not a midwife near.

There is this consolation
In watching the wheel turn:
We'll see great Herod cheated,
And a child survive again.

An Argument

With birds and dogs carousing in the sun,
I might mistake this frozen day for Spring,
Call that long icicle a swallow's wing,
And say the planting season has begun.
These outward signs, deceiving one by one
My senses but too willing now to bring
Time tumbling down, all gather and fling
Evidence of life, though reason says there's none.

Then who is right, the reasonable mind
Timid with past experience, or these
Outbursts of Nature, the birds' ecstasies,
The dogs' delight, the heaven and earth together
Kissing like lovers madly intertwined
And disregarding lawful winter weather?

The Dandelion

I am the sun's remembrancer, the boy
Who runs in hedgerow, and in field and garden,
Showing his badge, a round-faced golden joy
With tips of flame.   I bear my master's pardon
For my long, greedy roots.   I bring his message
And pay his sovereign coin for my passage.
If any call me robber of the soil,
Let him but wait on windy weather, note
How easily, without a mortal's toil,
I change my gold to silver treasure, float
The fairy mintage on the air, and then
Defy the curse of all industrious men.

Reconstruction

To conjure chords upon an instrument,
Be it a harp, or gun, or bombing plane,
Is to make human hands the hands of God
During the six creative days, which sent
The flowing shapes of music, fire and rain.
A fool can be a prophet with a rod,
Who, tapping here and there, will touch the rock
And make the living sources gush abroad
Till what were mirages will cease to mock
All travellers on that truly shadowed road.

Remember this now that the time approaches
To call the murdered children to their play,
Restore virginity to the raped women,
And change all lethal signs to toys and brooches.
To-morrow's task was ordered yesterday
By fingers on a trigger.   None, or few men
Dared to rejoice in death and walls crumbling,
Or hear in concentration camps the cry
From tortured lips turn from a hideous mumbling
To a defiance and a prophecy.

But so it is.   What we have done is done.
The evil will grow weary, the fool turn
From the blunt-fingered music of the gun,
And then the skies with other signs must burn,
Lights of an innocence renewed, a mind
With wisdom like the amaranth, which lay
Bruised, but, in the manner of its kind,
More fragrant still upon the seventh day.

8

A Sunset

These things are certain at the end of living:
The death of friends, and love with its regrets,
The insignificance of our forgiving
Even the proudest wrongs, and greatest debts.
We watch the flowers upon our heart-tree fade
And drop, leaving the twigs insensitive
Except to the thin music that is played
By our remorse, whose wintry fingers give
Reluctant touches to what might have been.
And even as they touch, they break the dry
And brittle stems that bore the maytime green,
Till memory falls, destroyed by memory.
Yet still we know, beyond that last forgetting,
Morning lies cradled where the sun is setting.

Thistledown

To grow lighter than air, to spread
Gossamer above a seed of thought,
And cast away, and be led
As the wind wills, in patterns wrought
By the wind: to be lifted so
Is to be born again, is to know
Life as the flowers know it, as birds
Feel it in their fragile bones
Lifting wings to the sun.
This is to live as a poet, who owns
Nothing of weight, but a sunshaft of words.

What Shall We Remember?

What shall we remember of this place
Where once a city stood, and men and women
Lived and loved?   Shall we recall the omen
That fools deciphered in an idiot's face;
Shall we repeat the words a wise man said
Before the dark events; or shall we think
Of individual things upon the brink
Of that catastrophe, dispatch the dead
Children to school again, and put the breast
Of some unmurdered mother to the lips
That do not bleed—as yet?   Or shall we best
Tell the betrayal in terms of guns and ships?
No answer!   Only the morning sunlight gleaming,
And dew-soaked grass upon the ruins steaming.

The Meteor

Such is this, and such is that,
To man's too-tidy mind.
He treads the earth, and studies it,
And has it all defined.

Yet sometimes he will see the sky
Seared with a falling fire,
And all his graphs are given the lie
By hunger and desire.

Then science with its dogma flows
Like water into sand,
And all that man has learned, he knows
He'll never understand.

The Historian

Here I sit before a scholar's fire,
While wind and distant gunfire mix their thunder.
Though it is wartime, I have my desire,
Which is to turn the centuries, and plunder
The past, for wisdom after the event.
Within the privilege of printed pages
I read how tyrants ruled, how heroes went
To a quiet doom, that grew in after-ages
Into the record of a nation's fate
Louder than battles.   And I learn how law
Has more observances in love than hate,
And on what strength a simple heart may draw.
To-morrow I may write of this, and show
Where present cheats of history will go.

The Microscope

Oh, Horror!   I thought I had it here!
Pray God the microscope is wrong,
And truth blurred, and out of focus.

First, I put a bee-wing there,
And saw the mighty cable, strong
As an iron bridge's girder.

Then, seizing on a word you said,
I set it there, fixed in its mood
As chemist dyes the atom red
That it be seen and understood.
We thought it was a harmless joke, as
The light pretence took shape.   Oh, folly,
To play with light or play with fire!
The word I set there, calm and holy,
Swelled to a shout of hoarse desire,
And showed the scaffolding of murder.

Omens of Spring

No hunter's moon, but a moon in March,
With icicles that clink and chime
At catkin-length on the budding larch
To ring the promise of pollen-time.

And now, to give false gods the lie,
Hunters range by day and night
To drive those evils from the sky
Which have encompassed in their flight

A haunted world that round the sun
Five times, screaming war, has rushed!
In the cold moonlight, one by one,
The ringing icicles are hushed.

The Gate

Here is the gate they told me of,
Below the hill-top and the promised view
Sunward and south.
It is a narrow place, of threatened ambush,
Last-moment treachery behind the rocks.
I feel the dew of fear upon my mouth.
A cushat-dove near by croons 'Hush . . . hush!'
Foretelling peace, but too persuasively.
I watch the empty sky
As one will watch who never may forget
How other wings have stricken from above
And left my comrade in my arms, his sweat
And blood sealing his last breath.
I watch the sky, the dove,
And wait the third remembrancer of death.

But that was far below.
Here where I stand upon the final height
Is evidence of labour, strength
Expended wisely, till at length
Conquest looms large and clear,
A moon upon an ample harvest night.

The battle ends, it seems, before the end;
And where the enemy should lift his hands,
No enemy is here.
The quiet air half drugs me; I have lost
The edge of horrors, and heroic deeds;
Lost the gentle things I valued most,
With innocence itself, whose needs
Dropped one by one upon the slope
Whereon I climbed and fought
The visible foe, and that invisible thought
Which battered from within at faith and hope.

Now I emerge!   The foe,
Defeated maybe, lurks below.
But thought has broken cover
And stands between me and that promised gate
Through which at last the battle should deliver
All the scarred army to the crest.
So where we might drive forward we must wait
In stony self-arrest,
Staring in wonder at the glimpse above
The open rock, the wooing dove,
Immobile in the victory of love.

The Meaning of the Mirror

Lift no hand: take no breath,
Until the waters of the lake
Fall asleep again, and make
A perfect mirror set beneath
A forest and a dome of sky;
A forest we may rove, a dome
Loud with larks, and pigeon's wings,
A world of quick and touchable things,
Where man and bird may build their home.

But if you breathe not you will see
That mirror drop in symmetry
A forest and a dome of sky
Where neither sound nor silence take
An alternate sovereignty.
In that shadow universe
Nothing warm may sleep or wake;
No bee to rob a flower's purse,
No man to come with sword or plough,
No justice with forbidding rod;
Not even time, with then and now,
To mar the second thought of God.

Legends

Will it be possible, in years to come,
When grandsons listen to our tale of war,
That they will understand how legends are
Most eloquent of battles, but are dumb
And do not tell of women's hearts made numb
With misery, of cottages stripped bare,
Of wheatfields trampled, of children made to stare
Upon the skies where murder's engines hum?
Time is a casuist, who loves to drape
Rock-scars with delicate flowers, and to turn
A plundered city to some other shape,
Quilting the horrors under grass and fern;
Urging a wren to build her faith-lined nest
Where once a mother wept, and beat her breast.

The Aspens

The aspen leaves are down.
Those trembling lips no more
Will touch our hearts with fear.
But with that fall is gone
Alertness of the mind,
A looking habit, a keen
Instinct, such as men blind
From birth possess, who see
The unseeable, know the unknown,
And need no aspen tree.

The Bomb

Some fool has hurled a stone into the pond
Where I liked looking at the clouds, the stars,
The underside of leaves, the little wars
Of midge and feather, or those between my fond
And harsher moods; for the mind will seek a mirror
In any surface that reflects the sky
And for a moment shows eternity
Shining through time, as courage shines through terror.

Now I see nothing.   The oracle is fled.
The little waters where all meaning sits
In miniature, lie shattered.   I watch, instead,
The mirror in my mind, where faith re-knits
The images that I have always known
Survive the fool and his disturbing stone.

Windless Day

Almost I hear the dying leaf
Unclasp itself and flutter down
To find a grave that knows no grief;
For violets have already blown
In fragrance on the musty bed
Where summer in old age lies dead.

So silent is the world that none
Dare sound a note except that bird
Whose breast gleams in the morning sun.
His privileged and holy word
Adds to the hushed earth and skies
A memory of sacrifice.

Moments like this, though they may come
Upon a mind distraught with sorrow,
Remind the sufferer that some
Mystery may redeem to-morrow:
Yet by their beauty set apart,
They 'll nearly break a happy heart.

Burdens

A song of burdens, such as press
Upon the sun, laden with light;
Or stars, with little less
Even when the moon is bright.
The burden of the trees, that lift
Each year a load of leaves;
Or flowers near the ground, whose gift
Is what the bee achieves
With lifelong labour, a dram
Or not so much, the piled-up gold
Of pollen being but fairy dust,
By human currency a sham.
The burden of the corn-stalk, old
In the ear; the burden of the sword
Weary of blood, welcoming rust
And sleep at the end of the fight.
The burden of man, forgiveness, the word
That weighs more after death's good night.

The Interpreters

Call the interpreters!   Bid them translate
The words the sunrise utters, when it turns
The ocean's rim to gold, when hills grow great
With light, and every hidden river burns

Suddenly conspicuous with swords.
Then for the second task to test their skill
Before the Tower of Babel, let their words
Convey the meaning of that sound, when still

And rapt, the evening sky goes down, and leaves
Below its canopy of silence, one
Defiant blackbird in some cottage eaves
Shouting of kingdoms to the setting sun.

If they translate these truly, let them tell
What Britain did before the doors of Hell.

If you will hold the jewel thus,
To capture the sun, or candlelight
Should there be no moon to course by night,
I'll break the future for you, discuss
Through fantasy the empty chapel
Of time that's still oracular.
By this deflection I will take a flower
Still armoured, still folded in its sepal,
And flood you with its colour.

Certain of evil, assured of good,
I'll prophesy such diverse things
As unborn children spilling their fathers' blood,
And beggars' charity to kings;
A Saviour on a Cross, who climbs
Down, and sets his name to crimes
That nevertheless shall justify
His sacrifice, and willingness to die.

Turn the ruby now, and see
The wounds of time drip from it.
Even so the chambers of the bee
In six-sided phalanx set,
Would drip with vanished summers, were they not
Sealed with that secret wisdom, which the priest
Dares entertain, in common
With the superb and unself-conscious beast,
And, some will say, with woman.

So is the stone ambiguous
Of all that has been.   I see no facet there
To conjure back what's been achieved and said.
In spite of all the cunning granted us,
We cannot stop the shrinking of the sun,
Nor by the resurrection of the dead
Know, as the Saviour cried, what we have done.

In the Snow

Past the shattered crossroads
Hidden under snow,
I am following the footsteps,
Tracing where they go,
Tracking down the footsteps
Crimson in the snow.

Shall I find the soldier,
Whether friend or foe,
Where he huddles waiting,
Hidden in the snow,
Moaning there and waiting,
Bleeding in the snow?

Pray God I discover
What I dread to know,
For my soul is crying
To him in the snow,
Woman's son or lover,
Whether friend or foe,
Dying in the snow.

A Homecoming

Now roll away the stone.   Let in the light.
Tell her that this is Resurrection Day.
Death having taught her, she will know the way,
Nor hesitate, nor turn to left nor right,
Guided by more than living human sight.
And if she finds our sunlit meadows grey
And lonely after those where once she lay
Among the dead, she 'll think she comes by night.

Must we deceive her so?   Have we no skill
To furbish up the sun, to gild the corn
And set the woodlands shining on the hill?
We must not cheat with those who come from death.
They have learned much since drawing life's last breath.
Theirs is the wisdom of the second-born.

This among the record of things lasting:
A song of joyful hearts, although they bleed
Inwardly from self-inflicted wounds.
But joy can thrive on trouble.   It will ring
Like bell-music between the clash of swords,
Confusing metals, and changing every motive
To virtuous intent.   Joy is the stone
That alchemists once sought, knowing its power
In touching baser elements, despair,
Anger, even stupidity, to gold.
And gold when fused from these, is currency
For earth to purchase heaven.   There is no other.
Wisdom and scholarship are not enough:
A wise man once was set upon a mountain
To view the promised land, and then forbidden
To enter there, because he knew too much.
And Faust pored over manuscripts.   But joy
Thinks little of such frontiers.   It sings
In golden mintage, makes its mark in gold,
Sweetly illiterate, and scarcely tutored.
Yet, having gold, and being gold, no acid
Touches it, of malice or cold morals:
And it will shine, in centuries to come,
Still virginal, still joy, among the ashes
Of hearts that took it with them to the grave,
Hoping to buy an immortality
For flesh and bone, and certain woeful deeds.

Looking

Look in your hour of leisure
And read its moments thus,
Knowing how time flows
Slipping through the fissure
Of uncertainty, of loss,
Of grief, and even of joy
Which is but grief's alloy.

Whatever be time's measure,
Its only mark is still
The quiet heart and mind
Which fill and over-fill
The soul, to leave behind
Disasters and events,
Chapters and accidents.

Study, then close the book,
And through faith-lidded eyes,
Timeless and blinded, look
Clearly on paradise.

Waiting for News

Waiting for news!   What news?
News from the darkness, how the seed
Should bestir itself in greed,
Clutch, consume, and break the soil,
Then, with no moment more to lose,
Stretch out, stretch up, and from that toil
With leafy voices claim to be
King in the forest dynasty.

Waiting for news!   What news?
News from the unknown, where the worm
Listens in its earthy form,
And hungry for what all worms lack,
Tunnels upward and pursues
The would-be monarch, drags him back,
Digests, then leaves for further grace,
A spiral in his royal place.

Waiting for news!   What news?
News from the light, the known, where man
Comes, as only human can,
To dig with sharp and shining spade
How he likes, and where he choose
In the wormy forest glade.
Waiting for news of mankind's will.
Waiting for news—but waiting still!

Peace-making

Let us refresh our friendship with magnificence:
Put by, for once, the shyness of division.
What shame is there in eloquence? The clouds
Have no reserve when over fields of corn
They stoop to the half-ripened ears, and weep
With joy.

        Thus you and I, two grains of wheat
Among the myriad heads seeking the sun
And heaving in the field, a fertile ocean
Of life, and further promise of more life
Enriched and multiplied, nations of men
Ripening to the harvest of to-morrow.

Come, pray for rain together. The sun shines,
And God is Light. But darkness and the rain,
The gracious rain, with the horizon clouded,
These come with peace, and swell the fruits of love.

The Lens

I will pause from labour,
And interrupt my grief
To make this moment happy.
For I learned when a boy
To peer through tears of crystal
And see the light enlarged,
While the small grains of trouble
With which my life was charged
Were magnified to joy.

Prayer by Moonlight

This prayer upon a moonlight night!
God of all pallid things, the trees,
The silver river gliding through the land
Like veins in a sick woman's hand;
God of all hidden miseries,
Brooding half in shadow, half in light
Upon the mounds and standing walls,
The thatches that with silver spears
Smoke in the aftermath of wars;

God of the doom that falls
On men made mad with killing and with lust.
Bring thy cool lantern to our eyes again,
Dim their red agony of pain
Till they, like her, reflect thy sun
In this our human midnight.   One by one
Let the brighter stars shine with her, shod
With silver for authority of love.
Make us accept this symbol from above
Our shattered earth.   Answer this prayer, O God!

The Promise

Standing on the cliff of England,
I looked along the sea,
And saw the lost and living sailors
In mixed company.

'Brothers,' cried the drowned and shattered
Sons of war and storm,
'See to it that our wives and children
Come to no further harm.'

'Aye, aye,' their lonely shipmates answered;
And nothing more they said.
But all the sunshine in the Channel
Love-lit our English dead.

These Words

These daily words you listen to, are not
One man's invention, but the growth of time,
Seeded from nobility and crime.
Some are blemished fruits, destined to rot
And fall.   Some revive that were forgot.
A few, like death in life, may faintly chime
Dropped from the belfry of a poet's rhyme
Upon the graves in history's burial-plot.
But all of them, long-lived or quickly gone,
Are active powers, the radium of thought,
The close-packed atoms of our human story.
Here then is need for caution.   Be admonished
To use these daily words as though God-wrought,
Magical master-keys to light and glory.

An Autumn Window

Look! Through this pane of glass
You see midsummer still;
Beds opulent with roses;
And up the wooded hill
Soft green shadows pass
As the sun sinks, and day closes.

Yes, Time's defeated here,
And the season cheated.
But venture out, the air
Is sharp and over-clear,
And something is laid bare
For you to feel defeated,
Lost, and cold with fear.

Poor Recompense

By city habits cheated
Of the music of leaves,
And the refreshing green
Of the linnet's wing,
I sit and recall
Summers that have been.

But thoughts are defeated.
Their strivings bring
No forests that sing,
No flashing, bright birds.
Memory grieves
In this handful of words.

Any Small Robin

This little fellow, blood smeared on his breast,
Stands alone in a world of tumbling leaves.
The winds of autumn toss the gathered sheaves
And strip the secrecy from every nest.
The sun goes down storm-harried to the west,
And sinks defeated.   Still young robin weaves
His tiny music, a pattern that achieves
Nothing; or so a cynic might have guessed.

But wait! That robin's song was overheard
By some heart-broken mortal at the end
Of all endurance; or it showered above
The clods late-shovelled over one revered
And mourned with grief impossible to mend.
Maybe the listener found new faith, new love.

The First Frost

Moon above the mist;
  An eastern star or two;
But daybreak's looming fast;
  Drenchingly drops the dew.

Then through that dew the frost
  Takes hold with deathly fingers,
And while the sun still lingers
  The whole of summer's lost.

A Bonfire

Here, in the frozen province,
Defiant of the snow,
Let us pile up the faggots
For other worlds to know
By our one beacon flaring
As a courageous token
That still we keep our daring
While endless summer lingers
In mind and heart, though bone
Is brittle and flesh broken,
And life is almost gone.

The Living Lie

When my imagination died
I walked and talked with men,
And seemed, to all appearances,
A healthy citizen.

None knew that bread and wine for me
Were ashes in my mouth.
Or that each day's meridian
Hung darkly in the south.

23

The bread and wine, the midday sun,
Those gifts the gods might crave,
They meant no more to me than if
I lay within my grave.

The day the soul has ceased to live,
Both earth and sky conspire
To toll the black obsequies of
The man without desire.

Wicked World

Blackbird, robin, thrush upon the bank
Where I sat hidden, set me thinking. First,
I asked which of four villains was the worst,
Three feathered and one trousered. Rank by rank
I summoned and reviewed their crimes, that sank
Past thought's horizon. One by one I cursed
As far as I could see. Past that I durst
Not venture. I left the commination blank.

Ah yes, a wicked world! I blame the Fall,
And unregenerate Adam with his wife.
Think what has happened since God slammed the Gate
And left the inquisitive couple to their fate.
But even so, offered a perfect life,
We four might be reluctant after all.

Something in Common

Stranger, may I button-hole you,
To say a word about the sun;
A dry word in a tanned ear,
Before each goes his way, the one
Northward, with a furnace at his back,
The other south, his front on fire?
Here where we stop, the cooling stack
Is still not cool enough to keep
The scent of hay from boiling over:
And by the bee that staggers near
I see that honey from the clover
Runs in the heat, and slips the sack.

I'll show you, stranger, how to roll you
A devil's rhubard to a shape
That fits into your threatened nape
And saves a touch of fever-stroke
(You going north) or any other
Mischief to the skin or blood.
Maybe it's madness to have stood
Even a moment in this flame;
But such universal fire
Is something shared.   We've had the same
Blinding experience and desire.
My way lies southward.   Good day, brother.

The Renaissance

This chill summer morn
Above the mists,
I blow an imaginary horn
Through my hollow fists.

It wakes the sleeping powers,
Strange gods and forces
Who keep the tides, the hours,
And the stars in their courses.

I see the forest tremble,
I hear the orchards sing
A louder song of joy
Than the lark on the wing.
And greater miracle still,
I watch beyond my will
Both mind and bones dissemble
The dancing faith of a boy.

The Treasure

This may be true,
To have so rich a love
That all the universe is gold,
And even the dark coffers of indifference
A treasury to hold
Against disaster, in lieu
Of this authentic, which we may not have
As time grows old.

Absence has nothing, loss,
Death itself, to make us poor;
Even this boast, so dangerous,
As life the traitor knows.
The more we lose, the more
Our wealth of understanding grows;
And if love at its source
Could die, what we have known
And held, and spent,
We shall in recollecting,
Thereby be resurrecting,
Making that Lazarus a monument
Of love's eternity, to call our own.

PART TWO

THE DREAM AND OTHER POEMS

1927

The Dream

EVEN the noonday sun has not dispelled
This cold dream of a murdered face.   The rock
Still yawns beneath me, with the pine trees felled
By earthquake, where the mountains interlock
And crush the torrent in a cruel ravine.
Still I can hear the evil raven croak;
Still see the precipice whose edge of green
Is torn and ragged where the struggle broke,
And one man stood alone, and one man fell.
Silence resettled on that lonely height:
Only the raven croaked that he would tell,
And the stream whispered infamy all night.
To-day I go about the streets of life
Waiting the vengeance, and the secret knife.

Mirage

I saw a man on a horse
Riding against the sun.
'Hallo! Don Cossack!' I cried.
He shouted, 'Hallo, my son!'

The Caspian Sea shimmered;
The Kazak tents shone
For a moment in England,
Then the horseman was gone.

The Sea

Now that the wind has veered,
And murmurs from the south,
I feel, though far inland,
The salt upon my mouth.

I see the foam, the surge,
Moon-harried to the shore;
The waves massed behind;
The spray blown before.

And I acknowledge now,
Though landsman from my birth,
This monster that commands
Three-quarters of the Earth.

Ascension

He has dug his ground
And gathered the weeds together,
Piled the roots in a mound,
Cleaned blade and leather,
Lit his pipe, kindled
The waste—and gone.
The blue sky has dwindled,
Shrinking after the sun.
The birdsong, dying, dying,
Falters from day into night,
And the homing wings are flying
To woods whose noonday height
Is changed by the western light.
The mighty trees ascend;
Scents float from the soil;
Tired labourers unbend
And go up from their toil.
Distant, sleep-born cries,
Night-signals, rise,
The moon rides up from the hill,
Floods forest and mound,
And falls on that smoke-thread, still
As a lonely spear in the ground.

Legend

They say he stopped his horse and talked to her
Some minutes' length upon the mossy bridge.
But that I doubt, for she has never said,
Since she was ill and numbered with the dead,
Whether he spoke, or merely reined his horse,
And gazed in sorrow over the balustrade.
These emperors of men are not so free
As gossip presupposes them to be,
Of speech with common folk.   They do not greet
Upon the road, but ride with fixed resolve
And that immortal patience of the great,
Which cloaks them round in sombre dreams of fate.
They are expectant people, waiting one
Who should arrive, to meet them on the way
With messages of some remote affray
Unheard of in the lands through which they pass.
He may have stopped.   I cannot think he spoke.

A stranger told me you were dead,
   And I, unmoved, replied,
Asking in even tones, the place
   And hour you died.

But as, half reverently, he told
   The things I asked of him,
I saw you on a summer night,
   With your eyes dim,

Telling your dreams to me, the hopes
   That would not let you rest;
The faith in life, the faith in love.
   I saw your breast

Rising and falling to the moon
   White as a troubled tide
That sweeps the world, but cannot find
   A place to abide.

Youth upon your shoulders lay,
   A cloak that made you one
With the luring beauty of the South;
   Warm as the sun.

Your hair was fragrant in those days,
   And your eager hands would touch
The empty air as though your thoughts
   Were fruit to clutch.

You would not rest.   One night you lay
   Sleeping upon my breast;
I saw the torment of your sleep—
   You would not rest!

Daylong, nightlong, throbbing heart,
   Wounded with life, you bled.
Now it is over; now you are healed;
   Now you are dead!

The Intruder

Quietly from the cottage door he crept,
And slipped into the shadow of the night.
But as he fled, I called upon him, 'Death!
Oh coward, have you touched them while they slept?'

The Shape heard nothing; only crouched and fled.

Then I crossed the threshold; trod the stair,
And stood within the chamber of the dead.
But when I looked; Oh miracle of breath!
The dark marauder had not halted there.

Bell Practice

Hark! They are ringing over the hills the peals of old England,
The octaves of yeomen, and staves of the soil.
The wheelwright pulls tenor, the old sexton the treble bell,
And the village lads back from the wars pull their ropes,
Dinging their music, their bravoes and salvoes,
Shaking the belfry till starlings atremble,
Chatter and fret with the clatter and rope-grind.

Now the paean is set, and the major's full clangour
Goes ringing—swinging—dinging, full-sailed down the octave,
Then up to the overtone, and breaks in its tangle,
Jangling and wrangling from bass tone to tenor,
Giants a-quarrelling, discordant, shouting,
Tumbling in the wind, thudding and thumping,
Till the woodside's a-shake, and the towers of the Hall
Rock in the deluge.   But peace! the wind enters the valley,
Carries the combatants over the hills
And whispers them there, a secret of evening,
While the woodlands take breath, and the cornfields sigh.

Then back rush the ringings, rejoined and rejoicing,
Shouting together so friendly and fine,
Running the octaves as sharp as the whip-crack
Of teamers at harvest home, proud of the grain.
Loud peal and paean, bourdon and burden
Swinging, one voice, ringing 'Rejoice!'
Tumble the monsters, the pride of the valley;
And over the tumult, slow steering and mounting,
The overtone thrums and hums, and leads them together
In the hymn to old England, pulled by her yeomen.

Italy

I read of Italy the other night,
And the old longing welled up, the old pain.
I thought time had quelled it, every year
Slowing the pulsing blood of that desire
Until there rested only in my heart
A quiet pool of colour—Italy!

But that security was false.   Even so
A gusty passion may die down, and leave
The deep-branched forest-growth of love in silence,
For years no leaf atremble, not a sigh
In the hanging fronds; all in eternal stillness;
Sleep—sleep—in the twilight of the trees,
Until their origin and native strength
Are half forgotten, so perfect do they stand,
So serene—the very world seems empty.

Then on a sudden there is heard, high up,
Over the furthest reaches of the wood,
Strange argument, and bandying of noise,
Voices of foliage, a myriad tongues
Loosened with fear, passing anxiety
Rapidly on, swiftly as flame, from bough to bough,
Until the trunks sway, and the mossy buttresses
Groan in the earth, and locked branches shriek—
Passion is loose again in the forest of love!

Ah!   To tread Italian soil but once!
How does a lover feel, who, virgin-hearted,
And fed with romance of an earlier day,
Finds on a night of June a laughing girl
Fairer than all he dreamed of?   How can be told
The lyric of his heart, when in response
To his importuning glances, he beholds
Her laughter subtilizing into shades
Matching the moonlight when its rays begin
To touch the fading daylight with a life
Strangely exterior, yet giving it
Magic for sleep, a soul to its extinction?
Such is the smile of Italy to me,
Coming across the waters from the South.

And should the June night aid him, would that boy,
Drunken on warmth that lingers in the grass
And perfume of the seeded hay, heart-dazzled
By western lights that, sinking behind the trees,
Make them cuprous domes of secrecy
Where oracles lurk, batlike, in their gloom;
Would he have courage to approach her there,
Challenge that beacon of the setting sun
Deep in her eyes, touch the Cassandra bosom,
That fiery-cold and wondrous unexplored,
That valley of the mystery?   Would he dare
Assault the darkness-fostering mouth, aspire
To deeper midnight glories, intimate joys
That should be a potion for youth, to change it swiftly
With the drug called knowledge?   And so, heart to heart,
Should they upon the summer night find rest,
Sink into the silence, and be merged
In the sleep of the birds, the darkness before dawn,
And the sweet chill air that follows up the stars
As they fade from the eastern morning; should those lovers
Wake then, and rise into the light of day,
Would they find the whole world changed about them,
Fused, like their thoughts, in passion's vast alembic
And so made unified and crystalline,
Yet changed and terrible with beauty, glowing clear,
The unforeseen Life's mystery in the midst?

And should I come *thus* to Italy, to drink
Deep from her eyes, as Leonardo once
Drank from the Gioconda, and thenceforward
Go more secretly about the world,
Hugging a deeper wisdom in my heart,
And in my soul a never-dying love
Richer than its beloved—Italy?

Allotments

Lifting through the broken clouds there shot
A searching beam of golden sunset-shine.
It swept the town allotments, plot by plot,
And all the digging clerks became divine—
Stood up like heroes with their spades of brass,
Turning the ore that made the realms of Spain!
So shone they for a moment.   Then, alas!
The cloud-rift closed; and they were clerks again.

Nightfall

A swallow soaring and dipping,
And a seagull crying.
These are the only living
In a world that is dying.

The sun is drowned in the marshes,
His light quenched in the brakes.
A shiver runs over the barley,
And the wild grass quakes.

The sea tide meets the river,
Their waters, without a sound,
Lock and wrestle in torment.
Night shadows creep over the ground.

The Ship

Swinging round into harbour
Came the ship.
I saw it through her blown hair
As we stood lip to lip.

The ardour faded between us.
Cold and still,
We watched the ship drop anchor
In the shadow of the hill.

On Tour

We should be on the road ere this,
    Drinking the morn with eager mouth,
We are belated, robbed of bliss,
    That hangs like fruit upon the South.

The summer day, with hours of gold,
    Has spent some, and we have not shared.
Sleep made us miserly and old;
    Noon must not find us unprepared.

Surprise, and dew, and seawind kiss,
    These are delights that will not keep.
We should be on the road ere this;
    The god of gipsies is not sleep!

The Tryst

The mist is on the meadows,
Breast-high in the moon;
And woodsmoke rises silver
O'er cold roofs of the town.

Now is the hour we longed for,
The solitude we planned.
But oh, this frozen passion
Was not by us designed!

The Gale

Last night the heavens were blown about,
Stars were guttering in the height,
The moon collapsed, and was harried out,
And an old owl, debarred from flight,
Would have shrieked had the wind not been so cold,
Chilling her rage, stopping her breath,
Filling her tree-trunk nest with groans,
Churchyard rustlings, whispered death,
Or seawaves dragging seamen's bones,
Bones that would ache were they laid in graves.

The sheep were huddled up in the fold,
Tottering creatures, half asleep,
Swaying together, their cold wits muddled,
Wondering what the din is about
In the world without, where the autumn leaves
With blizzard touch fling past unseen,
Tapping at windows under the eaves,
While the wind creeps in and flutters the hair
Of the sleeping children.   Ah!   Will it dare . . . ?
They sigh, and snuggle their heads in their nightgown sleeves.
The wind mutters under the quilt, and dies.

The night is so dark; nobody sees
The ruin, the flight of the summer green,
Leaving the stark and shivering trees
To loom in the starbright morning skies,
Bare.

The Question

There was light in the eastern sky,
And lifting of leaf and wing;
A wind that rose with a sigh;
When a bird, a trembling thing,
Quietly began to sing.

It was gentle, and calm, and still,
And shaken with lingering sleep;
Yet it lured the mist from the hill,
And the shades that night-watch keep
Fled from hollow and steep.

So much from the song of a bird;
Morning, and joy of the sun;
A song without reason or word;
Just a shake, a trill, a run.
Poet, how is it done?

Bi-linguists

Now I have learned the language of your thought,
Its silent words sit lightly on my tongue,
My self-communing lips.   Hence I care naught
For what you say.   I 've been where those words sprung
From secret mind to veil you in your mood;
And as I listen to their tripping speech
I hear the inward truth.   That understood,
I learn therefrom more than you care to teach.
Here is the danger in a faithful friend;
Never contented with the part you play,
He 'll seek beneath the gestures that you spend
On desert speech, discovering what you say.
The truest tongues are liars.   So, my friend,
I 'll love, but not believe you, to the end!

The Shower

So here we stand beneath the dripping trees,
The drooping trees, and listen to the rain.
It has been dropping now for hours, it seems.   The bees,
The flies, the rabbits, will never be seen again;
They must be drowned in the streaming grass, and thrust
Down the swift torrents, bubbling over the dust.
First on one foot, then on the other, we stand;
And sigh, and lean against the knobby trunk;
And catch the jewels in a chilly hand;
And wonder how far down the rain has sunk,
How far down to wash the earth from the roots
And bleach them white, and make the sap run thin.
All the world is filled with bogs, and newts,
Mushrooms, moss, and frogs, and boys kept in
Because of the rain.

             But look!   It is giving over!
The drops come slower, the leaves shiver and shake,
And a watery eye blinks out from the sky.   Birds wake,
The shadow lifts, the lark flushes up from the clover,
And the purple shines, and the green, and every stone
Glitters and flashes, and the road steams in the sun;
The butterfly preens her wings; the bee has already flown.
Good-bye, old friendly tree, don't you wish you could run?

Barriers

The strange world of the flitting birds
I am afraid to know.
The woodlands, with their leafy words,
The rustlings to and fro,
The furry inmates, swift and wise,
All evade my ears, my eyes.

But though I hear not, see not, still
They grow more intimate.
They must surrender to my will,
And teach me, soon or late!

The Recovery

When I walked out to-day,
I bore a secret burden in my heart,
A load of tired anxiety, the fruit
Of false ambition, and the mad pursuit
In which all men engage, who claim a part
Of this material Earth for recompense.

But as I went my way,
Bent, jaded, with each heavy sense
Cumbering my soul, not firing it with passion,
I turned a corner, and beheld the sea
Far off, across the widening valley's mouth,
Curtained with light that hung upon the south,
Dull with so fierce a noon intensity.
And plovers, in their wild and crazy fashion,
Wheeled and tossed, above the reedy bed
That filled the river, and hid its serpent strength,
Save for one shuddering pathway where it sped
Thridding the lances, till it came at length
To where the scouts of ocean flashed their wings
And lit upon the sands with foreign cries
That told of far-off splendours, and strange things
Waiting in their tropical paradise
For such adventurers as dared to roam
Beyond that line, where disembodied sails
Passed to and fro, like clouds by rain unshod.

So there I found the joy that never fails;
The silent speech with vast creation's God;
The morning Odyssey, the summons home.

A Morning Mood

Nothing unnatural occurred to-day.
The larks were singing while the trees were yet
Night-shrouded, and with heavy nightdamp wet.
The goslings stuttered in their foolish way,
Greeting the dawn.   Swallows returned from play
In the high heavens, where they had flown and met
The sun before his waking beams were set
On the hills, or ocean trembled in his ray.

But I, who chanced to see these common things
With eyes still dream-bewildered, felt as though
My soul had trespassed on the aftermath
Of the departure of those ancient Kings
Who came with tribute up a stable path,
And then went humbly back across the snow.

Frost

Still the retreating air files cold and thin
Up the moon-channels to her frosty light.
The wind, iceborn, has sighed out its complaint,
Rustling the oak leaves, few, and sere, and worn.
For miles no foot has stirred, no furry pad
Sealed the cold acres of unruffled snow.
Man has not passed, no wheel, no hoof.   The road
Sleeps quilted, sleeps beneath the moon, whose eyes
Explore the earth.   Branch-shadows follow her
Stealthily, moving as the blue veins move
Beneath the skin's night-pallor, when a child
Sleeps, and the sentinel heart keeps watch within.
Sometimes a lonely wing deep in the hedge
Flutters in sleep, and snowdust from the deep
Floats into light, and all is quiet again.
Only the stars are eager; fiercely bright,
They burn like hunger, prowling in the dark,
Glinting from icicle and frosted bough,
Illusive lights—cold, cold as death.

Ah! woodsmoke from the valley, bittersweet,
Scenting the air!   It is an acrid sign.
The curtained window and the yellow lamp;
Perfume, colour, warmth!   The night hordes vanish;
Summer is waiting on that cottage hearth.

A Death in the Village

It is quiet to-night.
The gale has fallen at last.
And the torn clouds' daylong flight
Is over.   No longer the shrouds
Of the bare trees shrill forlorn.
All the terror and struggle are past,
And the moon floats up from the hill.

One by one,
Symbols of work that is done,
The yellow lamps in the cottage windows gleam,
Warmer than stars, or far-off worshipped things
Lit from a human dream.

No song that a poet sings
Is sweeter or calmer than that curtained beam,
That light in the room where death lies down with the mother,
And the newborn sleeps, and whimpers, and gathers breath
And father and elder son sit facing each other.

Niobe

Oh stricken father; gather up your burden.
Your hopes are gone; this is all you have.
This was your blossom; now it is broken.
This was your laughter; prepare her grave.

Aye, this tender one, this child of laughter;
Could the rich gods give more to man
To single him out?   Lift up your daughter;
She cannot now run where once she ran.

The flowers will not raise their heads to her skipping;
Like a winter sun, their joy has gone down.
Will they tend her now, by the graveside creeping;
Will their fond roots seek her, and make her their own?

Gather her up; I cannot raise her.
She was our pledge, our four-years born.
Grieve, father; kiss her lips, then release her.
I was her mother; I dare not mourn.

The Cat

Hark!   She is calling to her cat.
She is down the misty garden in a tatter-brim straw hat,
And broken slippers grass-wet, treading tearful daisies.
But he does not heed her.   He sits still—and gazes.

Where the laden gooseberry leans over to the rose,
He sits thorn-protected, gazing down his nose.
Coffee-coloured skies above him press upon the sun;
Bats about his mistress flitter-flutter one by one;

Jessamines drop perfume; the nightingales begin;
Nightjars wind their humdrum notes; a crescent moon rides thin;
The daybird chorus dies away, the air shrinks chill and grey.
Her lonely voice still calls him—but her panther won't come in!

Ancestry

Were those clouds mountains, I would take
A thousand risks to scale their heights,
Longing to leave the hills I know
For stranger clefts where glaciers wake
Deep echoes through the summer nights,
And no foot treads the virgin snow.

But they are gone; the dreams disperse;
And in their stead the lowland hills
Of my familiar native place
Lie quiet, as my thoughts rehearse
The loyal past, and my heart stills
The inborn yearnings of our race.

The Past

Timidly she came down, stair by stair,
Feeling her way in the darkness.
For something had called her, someone—a voice—
She knew not, but heard it there
Out in the wailing darkness, the noise
Of the wind, the lashing rain, the groan
Of the agonized branches, and forest roar.
She came down alone
To the door.

With peering candle held before her,
Like that sleep-troubled queen of the north,
She glided down;
And the sinking shadows bore her
Into the well of the darkness.
Over the roofs of the town, over the river
Moaned the tempest, assault and lull.
She heard the deep wind sway the oak,
The ruffled ivy shiver. . . .
Again the voice from the darkness spoke,
Reaching her heart with dull
Insistence, moaning and dying.

The candle-light rocked and heaved on the spent
Last waves of the wild air-flood
As they rolled through the crannies and cracks of the door;
And the white flame flushed as with blood,
Gleamed lurid, and died into smoke.
She stood there, lame in the darkness,
And stumbled on words . . . 'Who spoke?'

None answered.   The house-walls rumbled,
The oak tree groaned in its roots, the vast
Ocean-flood of the forest swept on . . . on.
She wept as she listened, her tears
Stained with the dread and the hope of remembered years;
But the voice was gone,
And the door stood closed on the past.

Nocturne

See how the dying west puts forth her song,
Soft stars for requiem, hung bosom-low,
Riding like sorrow as day breathes her last
With deep-drawn sigh.   The wintry Hunter long,
Long since has vanished in his frosted race,
Calling his Dog into the south below,
Striding to fresh eternities.   The sky
Holds now but peaceful fires, beacons of grace,
Lanterns for mating-lips to meet, and eyes
To gleam beneath, troubled with prophecies
And births foretold.   The rustling creepers fold
Their ghostly fingers, cold with clasping green,
Round all things bared by winter misery.
The cuckoo lingers in the woodland deeps
Long after thrushes' silence, long after mellow
Slow, pouring, yellow-mouthed notes
Have died on the ousel's throat, leaving the air
Tumultuous.   Hark, oh rapt listeners!
Strange hands pluck at the forest branches, strains
Waft upward, legendary notes, and lore
Holding such harmony that beauty floats
Half unheard upon it from the seared
Heart of the nightingale.

                                        Ah! could they hear,
Those sleeping innocents, could they draw near
Even in sleep, what would their childhood thought
Construe from this slow agony, so fraught
With centuries of brooding? But no! deep,
Deep they lie, so late the night has grown,
Safe under eaves and attic, all their dreams
Garnered in other worlds behind the close
Firm-bolted eyelids; and the daylight mirth
With all its fleetness stalled behind the tread
Of slumber-pacing lips, that count the hours
In vital blood-pulse, as the souls within
Ride up and fall like ships upon the tide.

The tide! The ebb, the flow of life. It comes
Almost with visible waves upon the night,
This earth but jetsam, and our dreams but wrack,
Tumbling our music over, and our old
Familiar leaf and feather, voice and thought.
Hark! you mothers, and you expectant brides,
Hear in yourselves the lapping waves creep up,
Carrying others to the ancient sides
And shores of isled mortality, time-wrought
And garlanded with spring. It is through you
That beauty lives, you make the midnight sing!

The Newcomer

I lift her little toes,
And there behold
The daisy more chaste and cold;
A more virgin-fair primrose.
No prouder man can be,
When in her eyes I see
Sweet recognition glow.
It is a foolish thing, I know;
For the great Hand that wrought her
Made other babies so,
—But this one is my daughter!

The Purification

They have gone over, the god, the friend, the lover,
They have gone over.
It is growing grey now;
There comes the end of day now.

They were signs then, the stars were a glory for men,
They were signs then.
Those lights flare unseen now,
Things paltry and mean now.

They were true pleasure, the friendly trust, the praise without measure.
They were true pleasure.
Praise is an empty sound now.
Trust treads no firm ground now.

They were music, joy, and truth, the kisses she gave him in youth,
They were music, joy, and truth.
They are less beautiful now;
They are but dutiful now.

Aye, they have come to an end, the god, the lover, the friend;
They have come to an end.
The soul is alone now;
Strong, naked, full-grown now.

PART THREE

THEME WITH VARIATIONS

1928

An Echo

DEAR one, dear one, whom you are
I shall not say, for I know not.
The thousand beauties you have been
My eyes have seen and have forgot.
All the wisdom you have known
And shared with me, and put aside,
Even this attribute has gone.
For something of your grace has died
With every moment of our years,
Dying in birth of lovelier
Joys in joys and fears in fears.
Love with you is change.   Your love
Is fire consuming in desire,
A strange and dreadful power, a wild
And startled ecstasy, a pang
Of opposites grown reconciled.
You do not know your strength.   You take,
And take again, and bind, and break;
And lo! the shard of me that's left
Rings in your hands, both new and round,
Whole as a sword again, a bell
On which an ancient summons rang
Once, and is vibrating still,
Linking our lives with noose of sound,
Deep echoes of an earlier name
Sighed out at night in worlds remote,
Sighed out with joy, subdued with shame.
My ears have heard it, and forgot.

The Pit

As we stood swaying in the crowded bus,
I felt such utter loneliness, that you,
Heedless of the many who stared at us,
Leaned to my shoulder, just as though you knew
The same dark misery of desert thought.
For a moment thus we stood and touched the deeps
Of consolation, though we knew not what
The agony might be, save that it sleeps
And wakes, raising alternate hope and death.

49

The empty shores of time, with monotone
Of change and loss, suddenly lay beneath,
Mocking our dumb faith with their vast unknown.
Then we alighted, smiled, murmured good-bye,
And I walked up some Calvary near by.

An Illusion

When we met again I knew my heart
Was not deceived.   Illicit hopes and joys
Clung noisily round you, seven girls and boys.
And you, with so much wisdom to impart,
Tended those dreamborn children with an air
Of such devotion that my fantasy
Seemed flesh and blood.   Almost to my eye
Your unknown breast was tenderly laid bare,
Feeding the last of these unsubstanced forms.
I saw it cling where my stilled lips shall dare
Never to supplicate, or sting the fair
And virgin whiteness with love's gathering storms.
We did not speak of this.   We could but say
The little pleasantries of everyday.

Her Stature

One-time he thought she was a little woman,
And frequently would take her in his arms,
Dolling and petting her for amorousness.
But suddenly, upon a day of crisis,
She stiffened in the embrace, withdrew herself
And stood in a rapt ecstasy of fire
Self-kindled from the hard flint of her soul.
She dreamed a dream before him, of the past,
Mighty determinations, practical deeds,
And virgin enterprise.   The dwindling lover
Watched her with a horror of loneliness,
Sinking beneath her silent accusations.
She spoke, but hardly could he hear her words,
For she rose up before him like a column
Of fire, streaming upward into heaven,
Tiptoe, wide-eyed and flashing blue on blue,

Her shining hair a raven prophecy,
Her face a lantern of renunciation
Leading her on to chastity and power
To be a king amongst women, and a queen
Amongst men, and a draught of inspiration
To poets and the desolate-hearted ones
Who from the ruin of senses build new worlds.

Salt

Now having quarrelled and repaired the breach,
Let us praise salt together.   You may think
This but an attitude of emulation
Born of a worship for great Socrates,
Suspected once for the anonymous
Praiser of salt, who figured in the Banquet.
No!   You will not think so.   I know your mind.
It is familiar as my own.   They stand together,
Joint adversaries to rebellious passion;
Sometimes phalanxed, Roman shield to shield,
Against this northern onslaught of the blood;
Such blood as you and I have felt assail us,
The sudden treacheries and artful beauty,
So cold, austere, and yet not to be quelled
By the iron plaques and crooked arms of the mind.
And that companionship through war on war
Has taught us trench-truths.   Such are not forgotten
When shambles dry, and lands are ploughed again.
As far as mortals may, we know each other;
Having spilled the ichor from our wounded minds,
Mingled it, and there, upon the field,
Bandaged each other as we paused for breath
In the harsh battle where none ever dies,
But hacks, and groans, and bleeds, being immortal.
Yet oftentimes, relaxing, weak and spent,
We snuffed the sweat and crimson of the foe
And envied that rank heat, and the crude lust
Which all our weary and distasteful strife
Could not put back, but only gave more strength.
But we know darker truths than this, that reach
Past simple loyalty.   The treacherous taint

Crept from the foreign camp opposed to us
With songs learned there, that held the rhythm of blood,
And melodies of union.   Sudden doubt
Palsied our arms; minds weakly took to musing,
And wandered all unmailed up secret paths.
There followed fraternizing with the foe,
Whispered discoveries of lineage
Merging, and more immediate parenthood.
Therefore the struggle was not face to face,
Mind with mind against the surging blood;
But sometimes I would fail you, follow lures
That sang the mermaid's song, and led me back
Down all our human paths to the seashore,
Where once the slimy monster dragged himself,
Reared up, and looked on dry land with an eye
That wearied of the water-broken hues,
And now aspired to drink the light direct.
And sometimes you betrayed that aspiration,
Playing me false with fawning kindnesses
And sultry claims that were love's counterfeit.
After such mutual treacheries we now
Stand here together, having reached the sea.
And in our ears there sounds the sad reproach
As the dark, straining body, fin by fin,
Relapses from the shore, and sinks again
To those dull vistas of marine despair,
The trailing roe, and piscine apathy.
This is the bitter savour vain mankind
Shall taste at last, when all the grotto-potions
Stirred near the Spring, in Aphrodite's garden,
Have staled upon the tongue.   That ancient shape,
That ocean pioneer groping its way
Up through the roots of spore-engendered forests,
Was the first herald of the Cytherean,
Who followed soon, upon her seaborne shell.
Our minds have sipped the sweetness from her cup,
And are but cloyed.   Now let us drain the dregs,
Giving our heritage the primaeval tang.
Old Socrates was wise; he lauded salt;
And later still, drained a more bitter draught.
Come, love, be reconciled, and praise with him.
His final tonic we'll ignore—for now!

Catching the Bus

What? Only these few moments more together,
And nothing cleared; our very cause for meeting
Half fogged in this disturbance of our meeting?
This is too weak for tragedy, but tears
We share. Are they bewilderment, these tears;
Few, hot, and angry drops we drop together?

What summoned us, if not some urge within
Crying for union; not union got by kisses
And that thin prying madness following kisses?
That way would be dishonest, not mature.
No, not denied, but kept till soul-mature.
First, Order has to be arranged within.

Have we that? Scan your heart quickly—quickly!
Words waste a revelation; looks are swifter.
Dumb? Hear my eyes! Fasten there! Swifter
We fly, gazing wider, learning more.
Everything we've gained now. Failure's more
Than triumph; flesh flies as spirit, quickly—quickly!

The bus bears down—but now it seems sand-sunken,
Clogged, held back. The flowing river-water
Stands, and tipping gulls hang tilt above the water.
'Tis we so fierce in flight! The moment's gone—
Wise century! No word said, you are gone.
I stand alone here, travelled, tired, age-sunken.

The Search

Guarding his breath, he leaned against the storm.
    Midnight chimes were lost upon that wind.
He lit his lantern, set it on a form,
    Then wrapped himself in all that he could find;
Sacks, a coaching rug, a scarf or two,
    And over these a stormcoat, shining black.
Weltering darkness yawned before; a few
    Last leaves sped in the flying wrack,
Danced haglike in the circle of the lamp,
    Shrill and hectic, then were seen no more.

Sudden little treacheries of damp
    Creeping air, threading their way behind, before,
Tortured the candleflame to frenzied flare
    And smoky rages, half convulsive death.
But the vast floods of wind and massive air
    Flowed on above, leaving the ground beneath
Quilted with seeming calmness for awhile;
    And life returned into the troubled flame,
Brought back light, and made the circle whole.
    Then while he went, groping as though half lame,
That fragile ring of light would be assailed
    By demon darkness once again, and crushed
By invisible hands.   Again it failed;
    Then, moonlike, waxed anew as the wind hushed.
Up through the woods he strode, and on to the wold,
    Where the whin shrieked loud, and the ling whistled shrill.
He met the assault of the heavens, fold on fold
    Rumbling up from the ocean, smiting the hill
And breaking to tumult with uproar and shout.
    Crouching over his lamp as over a hoard
Of gold close gathered, and savagely ringed about
    With ravening hands of greed, he still urged forward,
Mocked by the tempest, stung by the windrace, spurned
    By the thousand voices of scorn that hummed and
        thrummed
In the wake of the storm.   But still the lantern burned,
    And still he fought, with mind and senses numbed.
'Where can she be?' he heard.   'Where can she be?'
    'Gone! Gone!' he heard within. 'She'll never be found.'
And all of the mad world that he could see
    Was a ruffled, shuddering ring of lamplit ground.
Then in the trough of the wind, a woman spoke,
    Crying her grief on the breast of a man by her side.
Slow, storm-battered, they drifted on, and awoke
    To the lantern's lurid life. He saw her wide
And hair-tossed forehead, and her pallid face
    As she leaned in the arms of the man, her eyes upturned,
And he in passion stooping, as though to trace
    Gleams in the darkness where their beauty burned.
The couple passed; vanished into the night;
    Shone for an instant, faded to shapes of grey,
Then vanished, utterly lost from that circle of light
    Where the mice of the house of tempest gathered;
Little flecks of air, and leaves from the fall,
    And humble creatures born of the lifeless dust.

The lantern-bearer still forbore to call,
    Doubted still that vision swiftly thrust
Into his flickering world of candleflame.
    At last he hailed her.   But none heard him shout.
The derisive storm returned, snatched up her name;
    And from the four sides of the heavens, blew his lamp out.

The Gift Withheld

Why do you bring this poisoned wine,
In your smile denying
The gift, the kiss, that should be mine,
Given in truth, yet lying?

Have you resentful doubt coiled deep
In the cave of your mind
Where the long-clawed memories sleep
Of loves left behind?

Some half-seared wound burns still?   Some swift
Shattering treachery numbs,
So that you shrink, and dare not lift
Free arms now new love comes?

Friend, cannot we together share
The unknown terror, confide
Doubts, lay uncertainty bare,
And stand side by side,

Dear strangers still, each half aware
Of dark reserves in each
Where sacred incense stings the air,
And love is robbed of speech?

Darkness

Now the last bird has ended, and the bats
Flitter and twitch about the hazel bushes,
Where the young green grows deeper as light fades.
Now falls the blackbird's song; a little grumble,
And silence gathers round him.   From the hills
Sleep comes, and westward droops and sleeps the sky.

Ah! very dim your face has grown—the rose
Is lost in ivory, the warmth in moon-colour;
And those eyes, that lately gleamed with fire,
Are sinking in the night, receding, luring—
But never to be taken, made to yield
Their secrets up with light, as the morning flowers
Shine from an eastern shore up to the sun
Who comes, sea-risen, eager for their love.

Oh, tantalizing love, thus to surround—
Even at the very crest and consummation—
The final joy with darkness—nay, to draw
Most cunningly, with subtle dexterous fingers,
Film after film of light away . . . first light . . .
Twilight . . . gloom . . . then fantasy . . . and last,
Where love should be aflame . . . maddening darkness!

The Rebellion

I. *The Question*

Stepping ashore, she looked at him, and held
The proffered arm more firmly than need be,
And he stood calm, not flinching, while she spoke.
'Am I afraid?' she said; and the sun-smitten water
Threw up its pale reflection over her,
So that she seemed to shudder amid flames
Of fire more cold than ice.   'Am I afraid?'
Then for the first time since the fever of love
First raged in him, he saw the picture clear,
Saw the first years of wooing, saw her again
As queen of those untroubled days, a wife,
A mother, unquestioning, and yet in soul
Still virginal, still stranger to the deep,
The dark, the terrible—love robed in passion.
Then he had come, and time had gathered round them
Stormily, signs and portents had charged the air,
Deeper the gloom had grown—husband and child
Blind, insentient, not one happy breath
Laboured in the ominous atmosphere that loured
On all the world, for all the world of friends
To prophesy the flash.   Those two alone
Went on their way oblivious, and thereby
Barbing the bitterest arrows against the lovers,
Wounding with faith, stabbing with confidence,
Until the maddened couple would have hated,

If hate had not been steeped in fierce remorse
And so dissolved away—only to give
Some quintessential richness to love's potion,
Which drugged these anguished lovers, filling them
With courtesies, and wistful moods of grief
That made them brood like gods above the pair,
The poor deluded husband and the child,
And pity them with an untold compassion
Half merging into scorn, yet ever falling
Into humility and shame.

'Afraid?'

He walked beside her on the river bank;
And the wide waters rolling to the sea
Took up the fear, and bore it on their bosom,
Frail featherweight, yet not to be submerged.
Then looking at her, he saw her shadowed eyes
Gleaming with showery light, such as in June
Will sometimes sweep across the purple clover,
Breaking between a passing storm, and one
Still billowed on the south.   Strangely her face
Showed to his love, that fitful god-possession
Which makes the dearly cherished more remote,
More unfamiliar than its casual setting.
And dread more deep than wisdom, deeper than hope,
Clouded the picture of their mutual years.
What had he now to offer her, what new
Tumultuous experience—she whose years
Had known the marriage-bed, and motherhood,
And westering passion sinking in despair?
'Fear nothing,' he whispered, stooping to her hair,
And breathing incense there.   And she looked up,
Saw fear reflected in the deeps of love,
And dared not speak.   Silently they went
Through shadow-pools beneath the elms, and crossed
Sun-smitten swards; so on through light, through dark,
Both with the painful burden of the past
Weighed down, yet bearing in their fearful hearts
The same, mysterious, immortal love.

II. *The Flight*

Beloved, can you hear me?   Take this lantern,
Turn it to the wall, lest the light stray—
Then wait for me awhile.   I must go back
For one last look at the familiar things
That prisoned me, for time has made them dear.

57

And there's a keepsake I would bring away,
And I should like, maybe, to peep—just once,
For the last time, at those two innocents,
Father and—O foolish heart, O cruel,
Cruel lover, coming with such enchantment
That I must rend myself, and live divided,
Giving you all my soul, but leaving there
The mortal part of me, the mother-heart.
I think all tenderness will die to-night;
I pray it may be so, for should I find,
One future day when we're in foreign places,
Lonely and homesick, leaning out together
From some high lodging window in the hills,
Dreaming above the mists and shepherd-cries,
Should I find suddenly my hand astray
Over your hair, in half unconscious pity
—Oh, that maternal gesture would recall
The little, wondering eyes, the quivering mouth
Pleading for comfort—a way children have—
For no reason, no tangible trouble, just need
Of solace, they having so little strength to bear
The burden of the strange surrounding world.
Could love sustain such probing of past wounds?
I have not strength enough to be myself,
Unchanged, and still susceptible to these
Deep mothering instincts. I must crush them down
If you're to hold me, happy and resigned
In the cradle of enchantment you have woven.
Cradle? No! No! that word is false for you!
For what have you to do with things of childhood—
You so mute, so passionate, so cruel—
Oh, forgive me, I am distraught to-night,
I wound you, dear! But think! I leave so much,
For ever! There, there, the lantern, take it,
And wait. Oh, I dare not look again—
No, I will follow you now. Take my hand.

III. *Still Waters*

This is uncertain truly, but the joy
Of danger lurks in every treasured moment
Like fear in beauty. Life would not be thus,
Eager, and pulsing, if in the heart's blood
The passion of decay flowed not, or death
Pressed not upon the cheek's flush with cold pallor.

Now that the agony of parting 's gone,
And the fever raised in body and in mind
By acts of counterfeit, day after day
In that unruffled house, where all seemed calm
And sweet domestic candour; while, in truth,
Dissimulation wandered through the house,
Tainting the food, giving the nursery tales
Strange innuendoes, mocking innocence.
That fever soothed by time and change of place,
New environment has fostered hope,
And humbled pride lifts up its head again,
And the heart dares sing its own song to the soul.

Do you remember how we fled that night;
You resolute, thinking you had all to gain;
I, creeping from the wounded house,
A shape half ghostly in my misery,
Shrouded with dread, and shadowed with foreboding?
Do you recall my halting, with the lantern
Swung at my wrist, and trembling as I trembled,
So that the candlelight shook round about you
Curtaining with unreality
A figure which already seemed a dream—
A dream I was giving up my world for, all
My heart's home—but I must not think that way!

I turned back, half relinquished hope—and then—
The wavering lantern gleam grew calm and still;
And the ivy leaves, with all their lacy frost,
And the silken spider threads, appeared again,
Just as the stars and a willow-branch are mirrored,
Lost, and then are mirrored once again,
As the wind's hand shakes the lamplike pool at night,
And then forbears, while the pool resumes the deep
Calm of reflection, stars and willow-branch.

So, in that stability of light,
Courage rekindled, I leaned down, spoke to you,
And touched you for my better safety, thus,
As I touch you now, with a timid hand
That trembles with memory.   You took the lantern,
And stood there like a summoning priest, a hand
Strangely and fiercely lit, uplifted, waiting
To take mine, claim me from the home which stood
Immobile in the dark behind us there,
Built on my oath; the walls my faith, the roof

His trust in me, the hearth my motherlove—
O God, let me not think on that!
                                    My friend,
Forgive this pain.   Since it must grieve you too,
I grieve for it; but no disloyalty
Lurks there towards our love-compact, that each day
Enriches and matures, as heart with heart
Plumbs unfamiliar deeps, to suffer there
Deep-sea erosion from the tides of the soul.

So paused I there, dazzled by mingling lights;
The soft domestic lampflame, kindly and true,
Ever at hand to guide my footsteps home—
And there, beyond it, distant starlight gleams,
Hardened by frost to diamonds' brilliancy,
With all their lure, and all their mocking coldness.
Which are you?   Ah, no, the analogy's false!
What safety had I there, in those dear rooms,
With husband, child, and comfort—and beside,
Dulling monotony, indifference
Creeping over my mind with deadly stealth,
Until hopes, joys, and griefs were all diluted
To half their strength by this strange nothingness
That crept in unperceived, as river fogs
Insinuate, until the morning sun
Throws but a hoar and dissipated ray
On a world that has no substance, line, or shadow?

Yet, strangest of all, affection lingered on,
And lingers still, a morning moon, that gives
A touch of fairyland to the sunlit earth.
Ah, yes, I'll call you now my midday lover.
You must have been dawn that came to me that night
And took the lantern from my timid hand
And led me forth to a life of light and feeling,
A high meridian of love and passion.

I hear now the rustling of the leaves
As we went, you with the lantern leading;
Then the opening gate, and my reluctant pause,
My heart still indeterminate, and then—
The quick catch of the latch—and freedom at last!
You left the lantern there, to burn away
And so be found extinguished—I dare not think
By whom.   Call that light a symbol, call it
The old love.   There it stood, faithful to us then,
Ironically lighting us to freedom!

Beloved, if I dared, I would return,
And I believe that light would welcome me.
For since we left it there, no adverse wind
Has blown upon it.   In your noonday calm
I have prospered, conserving all I brought;
And that compassionate flame accompanied me.
It remains now in the daylight of my heart,
Pallid, immortal, more lily-petal than flame,
Floating on still waters.

                              Am I weeping?

Panache

If you would rest, I have a safe retreat,
Cradled upon the midnight of the mind,
There you might sleep, untroubled by the wind
Of daytime thought, that has its fourfold seat
High upon consciousness.   The winnowing beat
Of reason's flail-like pinions should not find
Your wearied brain, if, trusting and resigned,
Into my care you gave yourself complete.

And is this love I'd shield you with?   Alas!
Such words lack countenance in these harsh days
Of disillusionment.   We do not know
What love, and faith, and duty mean.   We pass
A humbler mintage in the soul's highways,
So nameless my protecting love must go.

Neglect

He had not spoken for so many days
That she, in desperation, broke the trance.
She had been sick of body for awhile;
And cried, as women will between the moons,
For comfort, such as frightened children crave.
She cried!   But oh, the ghost she had espoused
Replied with echoed words and formal gesture
Whose nice completeness showed he had not heard,
So far away was he upon the heights
Of his own lofty spirit, where the snow
Shone in the sun of heaven with austere light.

'Is there anything to tell?'   She touched his arm;
And looked at him with hunger in her eyes;
Looked searchingly, with soundless eloquence
Breaking about her words like an ocean tide
Flooding in past a little human craft
Which gropes its way with caution, lest it founder.
Such was the faltering progress of her speech.

There was a depth of anger in appeal;
And jealousy, that bastard child of faith.
She came with these about her like her children,
As though to point her loneliness, and give
Pathos to her bewilderment.   But still
He did not answer; only smiled on her,
All gentleness, yet with as faint a light
As penetrates from those remoter stars
That some unfathomable universe
Lures on in orbits foreign to the Sun.

'What have you done?' she said. 'Whom have you met?
I want to hear these things, and follow you
Through all the moments of our separate day.
For you are all I have.'   And then he spoke,
Half warned by her impatient breathlessness,
As though a sunlit gnat-swarm he was watching
Veered suddenly, and then resumed its order
After that eye's-blink length of aerial chaos.
'All you have!' he mused, incredulous.
'It is not much.'   Then added this concession,
'What have I done?   Ah, yes, what have I done!'
Then paused, and smiled, and gazed beyond the swarm.

Confession Flouted

It is not true to tell me you are false;
This is your only lie, to say you lied.
I'll not believe your innocence has died;
Our passions were our only touchstones else.
Come, my friend, your blood with heightened pulse
Throbs toward mine, nor can that flooding tide
By thought of recent ebb be shamed, denied.
For can the sea, the sinless sea, repulse?

Cry rather, with a shameless fling of speech,
That what you did was swift, deliberate,
Chosen with cold intensity of hate,
Taught by divine perversity to prove
Whether by treading depths of hell we reach
Nearer some measure of the heights of love.

The New Evolutionist

Let us improve on nature, and extend
The bounds of lust by reason, making shame
More subtle, and refining on the game
Of ethics.   Thus do civilizations end
And spring, each with some newer power to lend,
Teaching the fire an added twist of flame,
Whispering to Earth that all is not the same,
That here 's a gift which she may take and spend.

Surely the God in Man would sanction this,
Nor chasten him for self-aggrandisement,
Bidding him wait, evolve with star and beast?
Only by this shall torment change to bliss,
The pilgrim soul emerge from banishment,
And hungry life approach death's waiting feast.

Misgiving

'Do you believe,' I said, 'that we did wrong?'
And all her answer was a downward look
And lips that trembled.   'Come!   Do you think *that*?'
Still no word.   And yet I read her thought.
I saw remembrance flood her eyes like wind
Filling a valley with its southern gusts
And lifting up the flowers until they spill
Perfume for very wantonness.   I found
No shame therein.   And I continued so;
Reading that face which now I knew by heart,
Just as a student knows his midnight book,
That he has pored upon, and made his own.

Thought by thought, like cloud by cloud, went past,
Each with its shower of half-remembered joys;
The first approach, the timid gifts, the words
Falling to silence, ere the touch of lips
Brought lightning knowledge of another world
Where men and women in the strength of love
Moved with the gesture of the ancient gods
Shaping the universe.
                        Then, after that
Review of great events, and swift assent,
She put the past away, and said, 'I *do*.'

The Laggard

If I should say, 'But you are late again!'
With what excuses would you try to quell
The thin suspicion lashing at my brain?
Some accident o'ertook you? Ah! It's well
To say that water, fire, and air agreed,
Sinking their ancient animosity,
To share in a conspiracy of greed
And snatch you from me with a miser's cry.
Or you may say some family of stars
Beyond the distant Pleiades grew jealous
And closed about you, iron prison bars,
So that fate willed not, though your will were zealous.
I'd take that harsh astrology; await you,
And say no more. But how my love would hate you!

The Annunciation

When in our midnight ecstasy we lay
Drowned in each other, suddenly there shone
A far-drawn lantern. Its beams danced upon
The interweaving waters, making play
Of broken light, that darted every way
Between the waves' confusion. I alone
Saw it. Ere I could whisper, it was gone.
Nor did I speak of it at break of day.

But now you rest your head upon my shoulder,
And hushed with joy, tell of that inward sign,
That concourse of the stars toward the womb,
Summoned by will of the Eternal Moulder;
I see again that lamp, and wonder Whom
It guided to our presence, yours and mine.

Intermezzo on the Viol d'Amore

Your love flames like remorse, burning me through.
We 've outlived passion, and calm thoughts pursue
Still softer, sweeter moods, as swallows haunt
Their own reflections when the day grows gaunt
And hollow over water, eventide
Draping the expectant greenwoodside
And hushing the disturbances of day
With whispered darknesses and shadowplay.

Such is our latterday communion;
The noon-fires canopied with cool compassion,
That evening verdure of the human soul.
So glows the radiant sunhead in the coal,
Set in the lantern Time; its decadence
Bringing the gift of home for recompense,
Hearth-comfort, and domesticated God.

For what is this craving for the unkempt, unshod;
This grasping against reason at the stars,
But the old savage beating at the bars?

Now we should say that poets and their kind,
Dreamers and primitives who lurk behind
The social phalanx, are not light-ordained,
But fools coquetting with the unrestrained
And lawless infancy of man, who swung
Lemurian ages where the forests hung
Matted and fungoid, overteemed with birth
In earlier days of sun-demented earth.
And we should hint how marriage was a state
Convened for safety by man corporate,
And shudder at the subtle thought that lust,
And sullen mood, and agonizing thrust
Of mouth to mouth, and limb to limb, and last . . .
But these are images of terrors past,

Struggle and spiritual paradox,
When mind meets sense, grapples, interlocks,
Both goaded by the same demoniac power
That makes the panther in the forest glower,
And chill the night's blood with his hideous wooing.

These banished, other claimants are pursuing
The channels of our blood, whose pulse is yet
Throbbing in ebbtide of our lusts' regret.
For now we find the aftermath no chill
Recoil upon the little deeds that fill
The story of our youth.   Instead, we grow
More passionate in mind as bodies throw
Their last and wearied effort in the cause
Of Nature's unrelenting nuptial laws.
Over the exhausted sleep of sense there rise
Souls charged with deeper lusts and subtleties,
Purged of pudescence and the ruins of pride,
That stifled youth when first experience
Proved love the serpent-twin of greedy sense,
Both charged with double-tongued inheritance,
One, wise design; the other, lyric chance.

We find the love-throes of the universe
Only the foreplay, as the gods rehearse
With sensual pattern, vaster schemes designed
To shake the various barriers of Mind;
Until one Joshua-morn of trumpet blare
They crash, and all the armied thoughts prepare
For the advance into the citadel
Of lofty self, where final secrets dwell.
What triumph then, to enter undismayed
Where statecraft of the first and last is made!

Mind is insatiable, and therefore first
Of all things being, by Life universed.
But like the impatient ocean-tide it creeps
Responsive from profound subhuman deeps
Darker than consciousness—to what strange lure
Of unknown satellite that moves demure
And virginal round some transcendent world
Which round a spiritual Sun is whirled,
And he round what? . . . We dare not tread that path!
But can infinity be closed in wrath?

We'll venture then, but to such mental height,
We drop the mind's equipment in our flight,
And from that transcendastral journey come
Back to this human niche, triumphant, dumb!

That creeping tide no mortal can turn back.
Creed and morality are but the track
It carves in chaos' quicksands, and thereby
Is shallowed for the twinkling of an eye;
When, with doubled decuman and surge,
It roars o'er its self-created dam, to urge
Its outer and its mid-deep swell to expunge
The momentary bastion, and plunge
The god, the law, the statecraft into deep
And monster-haunted waters trailing sleep.

Hark now!   I mute my strings, and shape my hand
To music that your heart will understand
Without the cold interpretation wrought
By that judicious foreign agent, Thought.
I am content to have proven with those chords,
Love's open instrument speaks more than words.

But, ere we sing the quieter things of home,
Let us rejoice like gods, that we can come
Through turgid raptures that flesh festers by
And emerge therefrom to this mind-ecstasy,
Whereon we see the impulse of our lust
Leap unassuaged and sweep the stars to dust.
The tide of life that shook our limbs, we find
Shakes now the stronger muscles of our mind.
Tossed in creation's all-consuming might,
Who can believe that death is pulseless night?
Twice we have fallen, in body and in brain;
And now our fortresses of soul remain
Solitary, facing on the flood
That rises past the confines of our blood,
Leaving those channels arid and explored.
What further onslaught will the waves afford;
And if the individual soul be shaken,
What eyes shall see the visions, what voices waken
The ramparts of eternity with long
Antiphonies of joy and echoing song?

Now, having tuned my intermezzo thus,
I 'll sing of children time has promised us;
And leave these questionings of life's inane
   To some more deeply star-bewildered brain.
Contented now with mysteries at home,
I 'll watch the strange fruits of our life-love come.
It may be, as they snuggle at your breast,
That mother-mystery will solve the rest!

Night

Leave me!   Leave me!   Let me rest
In the night's slow-heaving breast;
Kiss the solitude, and creep
Where the stars lie netted deep,
Shivering veils that half disclose
The warmth, the life, that ebbs and flows
Through the bosom which they fold
From my kisses, mortal-cold.
Could I touch that mother-flesh,
Freed of substance-veil and mesh,
Would the fever of embrace
Lift me from my mortal race,
Give my lips contagious fire
That should sublimate desire
Into music love-caressed,
Dying, dying, on that breast?

PART FOUR

MOOD WITHOUT MEASURE
A GROUP OF POEMS IN FREE VERSE

1928

Portent

THERE is no sound:
Only the quiet brittle of the fire
And flake-fall of ash:
Only the pursed drip,
Long drop, drip of water:
Only the sigh,
The high sigh of winter trees
As the east sifts through their branches:
Only the tramp, tramp,
And running to and fro of thoughts
Far away down the avenues of my mind:
Only that ominous gathering,
Distant murmur and cry,
Faint clash of steel:
Only that hoarse preparation
In the sleeping city of my brain.

The Dagger

Looking back
He saw the flushed ear,
The flood of pain
To the bosom,
The shudder
Of her shoulders.
'What did you say?'
She murmured indifferently.
'Oh nothing,' he smiled,
Going out.

The Chalkpit

One day they cut too far into the chalkpit,
And the top collapsed,
Carrying down in thunder and blinding dustclouds
A hawthorn tree in blossom.
Now those wide fans of springtide snow
Stand in the pit, unruffled,
Serenely dying.

Nodding

Here, by the hearth,
Sits ancient flesh and blood.
And lo! on a sudden drowsy nod,
The world jerks anew,
And the kaleidoscope of sense
Slips, slots, contorts to shapes
Eye never saw.
And a kiss becomes a crime,
A connubial joy
A spear thrust.

Earphones

Sound came sifting down
As I fastened the phones.
Music crowned the cottage.
The trees outside
Wrung their hands and cried in vain,
Unheard, forgotten.
And the owls
Signalled in their own world
Whence humanity had departed.
The ghosts of solitude
Came and went,
Blowing the logs to purple fire,
Sucking the flame for wine,
But they could not affright me
By my English hearth.
No latch clicked,
Nor door rattled,
Nor ivy at window tapped,
For I was far away,
Listening to the great orchestra
Bowing and drumming
In Germany.

Peeping Tom

As the last train limped along,
Carrying my tired body, and my mind;
The two weary of each other
After the day of labour together:
As the train limped along,
Sleep entered the carriage
And whispered sounds to both
To feed their sulky mood.

Mind acquiesced;
Felt her touch;
Slept.
Body turned uneasy,
Sought life still,
Peered out of the pane
At the housebacks passing;
And, at lighted windows
Saw nothing,
Saw once a gleam of arms
Curving up lazily,
Brushing dark hair.
Body throbbed an instant. . . .
Then turned back to Sleep
As the train limped along.

The Starlings

Trudging up the lane
One dank afternoon
Through a world of leaves and water,
Suddenly we heard the rustle and fall
Of a stream where could be no stream.
'Strange!' we nodded, 'strange,'
But spoke not; walked on quickly,
Called by the water.

And when we neared it,
The murmur and toss and flutter of wavelet
Seemed visible in the air,
Seemed to flow about the naked trees,
Vesper-waters and lavings of night.
And still there was nothing to see
Save, rank upon rank
Manning shrub, tree-branch, outer-most twig,
A multitude of chattering starlings.

73

The Bell

The Bell!   The Bell!
Who is ringing the bell?
There is no death,
No marriage,
No house on fire.

What alarum is this,
What king in triumph,
What gravedigger wipes his spade?

No! It is near,
It is here
With clangour,
Skull-clangour
Dinging
Ringing in the brain.
Ah, again! again!
The Bell!

The Flies

Is that old horse wearing black-rimmed spectacles?
Can that be molten amber trickling down the tree-trunk?
Is the bracken palsied
That it twitches, and twitches?
Are the cows ruminating on their outraged past,
That they suddenly lash themselves with their tails,
And, amid their daydreams, furiously shudder?
Is there a boy with a jews-harp
Zumming by the water?

Autumn Night's Rain

Rainsoaked is not dead.
To-day it means
Sullen beauty,
Angry colour,
Gleams of triumph,
Woods suddenly awake
Shouting a hymn to the god of berries,
The god of grapes:
And it means roadside pools
Quietly singing clear songs,
Draughts of light
And clarity of skies.

At the Funeral

They met again
At the funeral.
The bell tolling
Muffled them round with sound,
Memory, and gloom.

But standing by the brink of the grave,
And hearing the knock
Of earth on the coffin
At 'dust unto dust,'
Their faces flushed,
And they dared not look at each other.

So they bowed their heads,
And hid their eyes
With the mourners.

Preface to a Musician

Do you know how to begin?
Take the string or the reed,
And grow old with it in your hand.
Wake in the night
To feel if you hold it with freedom.
Let your mornings be heavy
With wonder if your suppleness remains;
And the day a long labour,
And the years a fear of stiffness.
Then perhaps towards the end,
Time frosting your joints,
You will make music,
Shake hills,
Drag men in their multitudes
As the moon drags the sea.

The Choice

They did not see the sun
Rise from behind the town,
Convoyed by a fleet of swallows.

For the grove where they walked,
Handfast, blinded with grief,
Was pillared and vaulted by fir trees,
Whose faded screens, hanging thick and still,
Hid day and night,
And the changing heavens
Plunging through seas of light,
Careless, jubilant.

The grove where they chose to walk
Closed over ancient wrongs,
Sheltered decay, gave death
A fragrance and twilight grace.

Handfast, feeding on darkness,
There they walked,
To and fro.

In the Railway Carriage

They dared not look at each other.
But the sun on the window-pane
Dustily burnished a mirror;
And they searched therein.

Into the flying woodlands
And the stream of green places
They stared, but saw nothing;
None of the flotsam and jetsam
That flowed past the train
On the river of Earth.

For in front of these facts that fled
Hung a golden mirage,
A glinting of hair in the pane,
Eyes cupping the wine,
The vintage of broken light.

Furtively,
Each sipped that sweet poison.

August

The onetime green and thymey banks
Are now grey-haired.
They are solacing themselves with convolvulus cups.
Too many, too many, alas!

For these white goblets of death
Have drowned all the former surprise,
The joyous variety.

Emptied, their evil work done,
They litter the pallid grass.

A Hot Day Coming

The ringdove in the clover
Shone smooth and sleek,
Taking her fill of the honey-tips.

Nothing else moved.
Clean and chill,
The summer morning
Brooded with prophecy of heat.
Only those iron dove-feathers in the clover
Flashed and smouldered.

Heavyhead

Sleepy one morning,
Drowsy in the murmur of buses,
The dull roar of life;
Heavy head on bosom drooping,
I dreamed, half dreamed,
Seeing and not seeing
Morning's procession from my window.

Just a figure coming into the room,
Yet not substantial,
Writing words with my hand,
Words I did not write,
Words which at waking I wondered at,
Troubled at the clash of two worlds.

July

How heavy the foliage.
Tree-trunks are stocky,
Like Atlas bearing the world.
Hills are brought low,
And valleys are lake-deep
Under the clotted green.

It has triumphed over the hope of Spring,
The many colours;
All that rebellion of flowers
Is beaten down
Under this passion of green,
This burden,
This marriage.

The Poppies

Like lips behind a veil
The poppies rest under the oats;
Lips parting in sleep,
As though night were hot about them,
Touching the souls they speak for with sensual fires;
These lips not petals.

But here it is summer morning,
Cool after the pride-shower;
The smoke goes up in prayer from the village,
And the hills are monks stooping under a hood of mist.
This is surely a virgin moment.

Then what is this fantasy of the poppies?

The Guides

As we groped our way
In the depths of the wood,
The little ivy leaves
Lying close to the ground,
Showed their smooth wet faces,
Lamp after lamp.

Dewpond

Wait!   Do not stir.
Lie quiet a little longer,
As though you still slept by my side,
As though the summer night had not grown
Big with dawn,
And cried out with a long cry, a bird-voice.

For the deer have left the shadows of the trees;
Are moving down through the mist,
Flank-deep, their antlers draped.
They are coming shyly
To drink.

Dominant

It was sad country.
For over the lupin fields
Shining blue to the blue sky;
Or over the woodland glades
Where pine trees leaned in the gloom,
Their last-year veils
Hanging like skeleton banners
In a dim cathedral;
Or over the hearth,
The ticking of the cottage clock,
And the rattle of cups;
Over all these quietudes
And domestic noises,
There hung the moan
And wilful grief
Of the sea.

The Four Kingdoms

The Man and the Lion
Approached from opposite jungles,
And met.
At their feet lay the octagonal Crystal.
By its flash and splendour
They beheld the Plant, a twi-leaved seedling.
Then the Man leaned forward,
Subdued the Lion's roar with a glance,
And whispered,
'Oh God, Your habitation is prepared.'

The Freight

Doffing her proud sails
As she neared the breakwater,
The queen moved through the harbour-mouth.

The invalids in their bathchairs,
Carefully breathing on the beach,
Cried passionately in their hearts
'Ah God!   What beauty!
Surely she is bringing me health,
New pride in life,
Swift blood,
And the bread of vitality!'

Then she deigned to approach her mooring,
And swung there, gently,
While the crew unloaded her cargo,
Chips of Aberdeen granite.

Nostalgia

I have read of Provence.

From the days of the troubadours
Down to our Mr. Wells,
It has been sung about,
Painted, and worshipped.

Oh, to be a successful novelist,
Or a newspaper-owner's mistress,
To have a villa there
In a pocket of the hills
Under the ultramarine,
And veiled with olives.

But no, I must be content
With the Home Counties
In Browning's England;
This little garden
Where the grey rabbits
Of Oxford and Cowley
Frisk and squeak,
And multiply.

Oh Provence,
Where I have never been,
How quiet you lie
In my dreams;
No flatulent cars,
No klaxon or hooter;
Still as your cypresses,
Clear as your songs.

Return from the Party

We came home
From the wireless party,
Where there had been a mild carousal,
Some extravagances before the loud speaker.
Then good-byes,
While she put on her wrap
And took my arm.

So we stepped out for home,
Late, and the wind low;
The moon lifting her tragic eyes
To the clouds frozen above her.
The face of my companion
Shone chiselled and pallid,
Stone under water.

I caught my breath
In the chill splendour
And hush of night;
Bowed my heart
Before humanity transfigured,
Touched with immortality.

We walked home;
Quietly, reverently
Discussing our money troubles.

Strap-hanging

Now that we are wedged together,
Sweet stranger,
Closer than man and wife,
Why not make the best of this indignity?
Let our blood rioting together,
Murmur stories of our life's adventures,
Just as a river in its course
Brings emblems from its source.

Swing! Swing!
We are shamed, abashed:
Thrown breast to breast.
You dare not look in my eyes
Nor I in yours.

And yet in spite of this
I feel strange sympathies
Bearing my heart back
Along some time-tunnelling track
Which I do not recognize
Which I never trod before.

Swing! Swing!
The crowd is wheat
Before the scythe.
You are swept off your feet,
Thrown against me, a wave,
Dashed on a rock.
But we survive the shock.
Could you tell me what you learned!

Could I tell you what I have!
I saw you in the sunshine, a little girl
Sitting on a gate by a farmhouse yard
Eating blackberries out of a handkerchief.

But that must be twenty years ago,
For your face was different then.
Ah!   What a relief,
One or two men
Are getting up to go!
It was not this face

Somewhat pallid with the City.
Time's disgrace
Had not touched it, nor Pity.
But still it was the same.

I do not want to know your name.
We are touching here by chance,
Some experiment of Fate.
Life has barriers, I know.
But was it you upon that gate?
Tell me, tell me ere you go!

But she is gone, without a glance!

The Alchemist

The sheet of writing paper
Slowly became a leaf of gold,
Changing under my hand.

I looked up,
And close about the window
Saw soft mallets of fog
Thudding upon the sun;
Saw him cool from fire to bronze,
To aluminium,
To water,
And vanish.

An October Gift

Here is a gift,
A gleaming horse-chestnut
Fresh from the pod.
Imagine it the first
Thudding on turf in Eden.
Ah Eve!   My Eve!
Your eyes are shining
Bedewed with wonder,
Bright as my gift!

Foreground

Behind the pencils of the broom,
The woods and distant hills
Hovered.
The town beyond
Was an uncertain mist
Trembling in air.
Only this hand of spikes
Earth-rigid,
Stood as a body for thought.

Quiet

The night was so quiet
That the hum of the candle burning
Came to my ear,
A sound of breath drawn through a reed
Far off.

The night was so quiet
That the air in the room
Poised, waiting to crack
Like a straining
Stick.

The night was so quiet
That the blood and flesh,
My visible self sunk in the chair,
Was a power-house giant, pulsing
Through the night.

Respite

All day the wind moaned,
And the trees flung up their hands in dismay,
Battling with their cloaks.

But after sunset,
The scholar climbed to the hill-top,
Sat down before the splendour,
And read his book unruffled.

The marshes stretched below him
Written over with mist,
Calm, unchanging figures of night.

He read that page also,
His idle fingers
Plaiting the grasses.

Removal

Out of the dark street
Where for ten years,
Poor and humiliated,
They huddled;
Sudden courage called,
And the lovers arose,
Found a cottage on a green knoll
Laughing ruddily to the sun.
There, joyous in strength,
Truly now man and wife,
In song they created
Children of light and thought.

The Last Phase

The town lights by the river
Were a row of spears upright.
And the crumbled moon
Sank,
Fenced by those quivering shafts.

No mortal would dare
Tread that camp
Where the desperate gods
Stood guard,
Watching the death
Of their queen.

Window-dressing

The bare trees in moonlight
Were giant stalks of lavender,
Dusty blue.

Silent and still
They stood against the velvet,
The unswaying curtain
Of purple.
Dusty blue; purple;
And, pinning them,
A red-hafted planet.

Powerless

Days after our talk,
I saw her sitting,
Drooping over the fire.
The injection of courage
Was losing its strength.
What was to be done;
What swift action
To kindle her again?
You cannot talk twice.

Who Whistled?

Someone was whistling.
Who was it?   Who was it?
Of the passing faces,
The tired brains?
Where was the demon of merriment lodged?

Over the drumming of the City,
Over the yawn of the lunch hour,
Over the pounding of the heatwave,
The boy-flute rose;
A lark from the dew,
A cup from the well,
A gift from a child.

It poised,
Trembled;
Poised,
And fell.
And the buses ramped on,
And the faces closed.
And the brains slept,
In the City.

Housing Scheme

All summer through
The field drank showers of larksong;
Offering in return
The hospitality of grasses,
And flowers kneedeep.

Over those wide acres
Trooped the plovers,
Mourning and lamenting as evening fell.
From the deep hedgerows
Where the foam of meadowsweet broke,
The rabbits and mice
Peeped out, and boldly sat in the sun.

But when the oaks were bronzing,
Steamrollers and brickcarts
Broke through the hedges.
The white-haired grasses, and the seedpods
Disappeared into the mud,
And the larks were silent, the plovers gone.

Then over the newlaid roads
And the open trenches of drains,
Rose a hoarding to face the highway,
'Build your house in the country.'

This garden
Stands unkempt, a disgrace
Amongst its neighbours.
And the house too;
Boys have stoned the windows,
And a few slates are loose.
It looks like a blinded war-victim.

But June has touched the desolation;
For the grass swings kneehigh,
Bowing powdered heads in the breeze;
The trees are dressed cool green, robed and crowned.
And there, in the angle of the fence,
Is a clump of willowherb, like a sheltered city of spires
Seen far off in the evening sunshine, after rain.

S. R.

The electric train growled on,
Its fangs flashing under the arc-lamps
That stood baiting it along the high courses through the town.

And the power-house beyond the river
Burned with the lamps of recognition in its hair;
Its four horns thrust up into the shreds of the sunset;
Demoniac, yet standing foursquare and lumpish,
Ceaselessly thrusting forth its brittle and crackling vitality
Through the level steel roads, up the raised nerves of the lamps,
And round, and round, and round, within the belly of the goaded train.

The Seal

Throb, throb from the mixer
Spewing out concrete.
And at the heads of the cables
Stand the serpent-warders,
Sweating and straining,
Thrusting those cruel mouths to their prey.

Hark how the steel tongues hiss
As they stab.
The men sway under the effort,
And their eyes are bloodshot with the din,
The clatter that shatters the brain.
Throb, throb from the mixer
Spewing out concrete.

The crowd stands by
Watching the smoothers;
Fascinated by the flat, wet levels
Of newlaid cement.
See how those curdled lakes
Glisten under the sky,
Virginal.

Then the dusty air suddenly divides,
And a pigeon from a plane tree
Flutters down to bathe its wings in that mirage of water.

But deceived, and angry,
Bewildered by the din,
The throb, throb from the mixer
Spewing out concrete,
It backs upon its wing,
Threshes air, and is gone.

But there, in the deflowered bed,
Is the seal of its coral foot,
Set till rocks crumble.

The Summons

At that moment,
Standing deep in the drift of beechleaves;
Windtossed, stung by scarlet waifs,
Snatched at by woodsmoke;
Suddenly piano-music
Woke us from this acrid trance,
Called us back to the house
And the first autumn fire.

Warming our hands, chafing our hands,
We listened to the riot of joy,
Stooping to the unfamiliar flame on the hearth,
Warming our hands.

Leaving the theatre
Through the litter of laughter
And the lees of mirth,
We saw the wolf again,
And the familiar huntsman too.

I heard you shudder into your cloak.
Crying a glance at you,
I felt the spasm of pain
As you looked, recognized both.
Ah brave!   Brave to say only
'It is cold . . . coming out!'

The Warning

Swallows still haunted the aerials and eaves;
And the billowing clouds of Michaelmas blooms
Rang with bee-traffic.
Late butterflies staggered through the low sunbeams,
Lingering under their drowsy warmth.
All the world was green and sedate,
No fever in the beeches, no fire in the elms.

Not until the sun
Had slipped quietly, too quickly, down the evening,
Did treachery show its cold hand.

Not the glowworm
In her grassy vault;
Not the moonlight
Weighing on the foliage and heavy fans of the trees,
And dwarfing the distant hills;
Not in these lay the foreboding.

But in that glitter of stars,
And shrinking of the air,
The teeth of death
Proferred their kiss.

Waiting

While I waited,
The orchard-tinted bricks glowed
As the westward sunlight
Crept up them quietly,
On its heaven-circling cast
Over to the world's rim.

Their tinges faded then
From pippin to sallow,
And I turned my face from the sadness,
The gloom that crept over them.
Faith grew thin,
And waiting seemed a fool's hope.
But in spite of the fall of light,
And the sense of loss,
I waited.

Time-fantasy

Ah, to get away
Out of Whitehall into an upland valley
A green cup between hills.
Then to escape that simplicity
And to win back the exhilaration
Of office and intrigue!
Any where out of the present,
This place, this time,
Any where that has the permanence
Of a childish desire,
The dream of a boy.

Under the Poplars

No word spoken.
Just a touch of your cold hand
Groping for my face in the darkness;
A kiss blown astray
Like a dead leaf
Alighting on the lapel of my coat—
And then you were gone.
The whip-clean poplars
Sighed together,
Flicking the stars.

Sunstroke

What with the gold of the buttercups,
And the marguerites scattered along the railway banks
Like a million halfcrowns,
I feel that surely the world is a little crazy,
Or that the wine of the sunshine has gone to my head,
And made me foolishly optimistic
About the opulence of things,
And that this ridiculous extravagance and flaunting of wealth
Is just a hungry dream.

Winter Sun

In the shadow of the haystack
The ground lay under a mail of frost.
But round the open field
The fingers of the sun had crept,
Unlacing the steel;
And the olive-skinned grass
Glowed in the misty beams,
Brave as a gipsy's coat.

The Loss

Now she is dead,
I know the grave is warm with beauty.
For though she gave, and gave again,
The rich splendour, and the tenderness
Lingering, piercing;
Yet always, afterwards, she shone
Undimmed, still as inscrutable,
Alluring me.

The glory she withheld,
The inspiration of humility,
The treasure no lover could spend
Except he had the greed of a god;
Who is enriched now with them,
Who takes those caresses with worship,
Those wordless confidences,
And subtle joys?

I have known her; I have been nourished;
But Oh, I am hungry still,
I would rob the grave,
And snatch back her tribute to Death.

PART FIVE

THE GLANCE BACKWARD

1930

ALLEGRO

The Choristers

ALL the spring day long
The multitude of birds made song
In the purple elms
And the flaming bushes.
The little crocus voices rang
Singing from the happy grass.
Then came momentary hushes,
When grass, wing, and feathered throat
Paused in rapt ecstasy,
Self-silenced in wonder at the sky,
The blue profound
With elfin April clouds afloat;
Paused as though content
With the caress of the living firmament,
The kiss of sunshine, tangled hair of light,
That touched and caught
Twig and cusped leaf
In tangle, kiss, caress,
Until they trembled into loveliness.

But from that trough of silence,
That momentary ebb of wave,
Sullen almost, as of summer noon,
The skylark sprang, admonishing
The feathered army, with shrill
Sheer drunkenness of will,
To sing renewal, to sing
Spring and daylong morning.
Then from the flowering boughs there sprang
Uprising from that rhythmic swoon,
The whole army of song.
It rose and rang
From tree-height and thicket,
Echoing down from the dome
Of the blue with a fullness of joy,
Young as the shout of a boy
Tumbling out from home
To the open green and the wicket.

Water Music

As our boat, reflected
In the mirror of the lake,
Cracked the mirror, crisply pressing
Forward, with a widening wake;
You looked down, and saw erected
In the deeps before our prow,
A world of weeds caressing
Sandy slips and crater springs,
Grottoes, water-rings,
Shades that flashed a fin,
Broke the surface, then were gone
Where the willow-fronds dipped in.

Slowly oared we on;
Gravely sweeping, like a cloud
Over the green world below;
Lapping, lapping, soft and loud,
Loud and soft, against the flow,
Crimping through the lipping ripples
O'er that water-forest looming,
While our shadow deep and glooming
Crept along the weedy bed.

Minnow shoals turned and fled
Swiftly, all as one, a single thought
Out of silver liquid wrought.
Pike, with stately heaving breath,
Vanished, slow and swift as death.
You looked down and viewed these things
As an eagle in his flight,
Poised upon astonished wings,
Stares at earth through floors of light.

The Sunrise

Ah!   It was good to rise
   And watch, above the wold,
The king with fiery eyes
   Stride as of old.

Gone was the lonely doubt
   Which the night wrapped me in:
Here was a foeman stout,
   Here was a crown to win!

Shape

Ah!   Looking down, looking down,
What may we see; what may we not!
Suggestion on the wind has blown.
The fruit is there; the fruit must rot.

What is mere shape that it should bring
Blood-pulse upon the heart, and change
A mood into a living spring
Whose waters through the world must range?

In shape such strength, what shall the Thumb
Who moulds, when it has ceased to mould?
They see, to whom sweet sound is dumb,
They hear, to whom the sun is cold!

Snowscene

There were soft sounds,
The pineboughs sloughing their snow-sheathes,
Snow sloping to snow on the skirt of the forest;
No one to see it, the quiet drama,
Winter's afterthought, following the blizzard.

The patter of gulls' feet on the ice
Was another sound.

These were all; for the world,
Folded, furled, closebound,
Slept on, in the spell of the wizard,
Breathing as a mother breathes,
Feeding her child.

Solstices

Worship the summer sun
In the high heavens burning,
While the wheat-filled earth
Ripens, slowly turning
Her swollen sides to his beams,
Until her bosom teems
With multitudinous birth.

Worship him then, but love
His level winter rays,
That through shy fireside days
Cool and discreetly move,
With curious fruitless care
Treading the inner air
Of cavern, house, and den,
Companion to mouse and men.

Field-history

Speaking with one of the Danes
Who inhabit Suffolk,
I asked this descendant of giants,
'Where are your blue eyes?'

'Gone,' he said, 'Gone!
Rusted with sojourn
On English clay.'
Then he stiffened to plough.

From the South

The wind from the south
With her lovely mouth
Sang to the weary trees,
'Sad are your memories,
But I have known sadder;
I come from the ocean,
Which is wilder and madder,
More rebellious than earth.
But oh, my lovely ones,
Giving your grace to death,
Hark how my sighing breath
Is yet dewy with mirth.
I know your loneliness;
Through crimson and brown you turn,
Tragic in your distress.
I have a prophecy.   Learn!
Learn of my melodies;
No beauty ever dies.

All that you cast from you,
All that is torn from you,
Forlorn and most beautiful,
Strewn on my bosom and
Cast on the weeping skies;
All that you lose is given
Back to the womb of heaven,
Deep in the winter dun
Buried, to wait the sun.
Sleep then, be dutiful,
Joy will return.'

Endymion by Day

Feel how the breeze
Stoops to the arms
Of the plane trees,
Swoons to their charms
In the heat of noon,
While the doves croon.

Would you not lie
Invisible, a ghost,
A movement, a sigh
Shuddering, lost
In my body's length,
In my soul's strength?

Thus the moon-queen
To a sleeping lad
Came for love, unseen,
Gave all she had;
While he, it seemed,
Still slept and dreamed.

Pause on the Road

All day the rain was dripping from the leaves;
All day, all night, the trees were dark with rain.
Sigh followed sigh; speech like a winter sun
Grew thin and faded into watchfulness.
A wary silence settled on our minds,
A mist of thin suspicion. I broke the veil,
Sending unguided words along the stream.

'Are you sleeping; has your heart grown weary
Of struggle, of the fierce desire for knowledge,
A high companionship along the road
Uphill, toward the wider view of the world,
Sunspaces, realms of cloud, labouring valleys,
And the mountains sleeping under moon and sun
By night and day where the austere gods of thought
Brood in annihilating loneliness?'

Then for reply you turned aside, and wept
Tears that were blind, not knowing of their birth.
'Ah! Tell me who you are!' I heard you say.
'Close, blood-mingled, sense to sense, yet strange,
Grown suddenly strange and unfamiliar.
Whose voice is this that was the voice of love,
So intimate that all my body trembled
When you spoke?'
                        'I do not know,' I said,
And touched you shyly, with a hand of wonder.
'Here is the faith of love,' I whispered, 'Here,
While passion sleeps, and understanding hides
Its head.   Maybe love is only courage.'

When you looked up, the raindrops caught the sun,
And the wet trees were glittering with light.

The Meteor

Night was not dark enough; I saw
    The mansion of your eyes
Lit with a spiritual law
    And a subdued surprise.

There with the sombre stars, and deep
    As their unshaken hordes,
I saw your resolution sweep,
    And vanish into words.

The Builders

They did not speak, but walked beside the lake
Watching the wild duck flying low to water
Touched by dropped wings to spray of molten bronze
Against the autumn sunset.   Veiled in smoke,
And netted in the rain of shrunken leaves,
Day died, and with it died the ghost of summer,
The wistful light, false warmth.

                           They did not speak,
These lovers who had brought the harvest in,
Watched through the autumn over deeds of spring,
And now were rich.   They had no need for speech,
But took their way in thankfulness, their eyes
Half veiled, drooping to keep the world away,
Guarding their joy and their increasing wonder
At this dark miracle of fruitfulness
Amid a universe of failing powers,
The ageing year, the old and tottering sun,
The memory of death, youth snatched away,
And beauty steadily bereaved by time.

Such was the world they trod, a world of ashes,
A ruined hemisphere, yet lifted up
In the calm strength and glory of this love,
Renewed in death because these mortal hearts
Had sworn a troth against their dying blood,
And now were strong to cradle life itself;
With their frail hands, and intuitive faith,
Building a deathless summer in their souls.

July Sabbath

Only the chitter of sparrows
In the silent village;
And the little surf of the rain
Mellowing the Sunday bell.
It is very quiet here; it is quiet
In the deep pause of summer,
Before the gathering of fruit.
It is the sleep after sowing;
The Sabbath of Hope.
Speechless with thanksgiving
Is the heart of the village.

The Watermill

'Birth . . . marriage . . . death;
Sorrow . . . joy . . . sorrow.'
So murmur the mill waters,
Turning the wheel beneath.
To-day and to-morrow,
These are here and coming,
The fall and foaming.
The quiet lies behind
In the deep mind,
The gathering strength,
The tree-haunted deep
Which tumbles at length
Over, over again
Into life out of sleep,
Grinding the grain.

Clumsy

I had not turned the petrol off, I thought;
Forgotten to lock the wash-house door for the night;
So I went out again, and fumbling, sought,
Already half asleep, to put things right
And snug.   Covering the radiator with a rug,
I clashed the garage door.

                   Then suddenly,
Silence came home to me with a wounded cry,
Hurt by my clumsiness.   The glaring fault
Loomed heinous in the night; rang from the beechwood,
Re-echoed from the little railway-halt
And stopped the singing of the nightingale.

I stood ashamed, exposed in the moon's flood.
I bowed my head, grieving as silence bled,
And there, heart-torn, and from my passion pale
I worked the miracle, reclaiming from the dead
This dying mystery, this queen of thought,
This bride of night and mother of solitude.
For as I stood I quelled my very blood,
Stilled its riot; then, tired and overwrought,
Listened.   Silence was healed.
                  I crept to bed.

Am Meer

Sitting in the boat's prow
Behind the dividing waters,
We were one in thought and vow,
Silent as the arrow-shaft.
Never lovers then, but rather
Single weapon forged and thrust
Flying from the string, whose thrumming
Sung behind us still,
Rung behind us, shrill with challenge,
Swifter than the murmuring sweetness
Born of mingled songs of lovers,
Closer, crueller, one and deathly,
Your will and my will.

The Birth

Only the cricket chirps; no nightingale
Floods the deep hour of darkness with her song.
Earth with her lovely burden in her womb
Labours in whispered pain, and staggers pale
In star-watched agony.   Not long!   Not long,
Oh Mother; even now the moments loom,
And the moon-midwife with her lethal lamp
Searches thy deathlike bosom for a sign.
With birth-dew now thy shrouded hair is damp.
Hasten, Oh God! complete this work of Thine!

Simplicity

They are so many, man's grim miseries.
His brain is sullen with a thousand scars;
Curtains of ambition blind his eyes
To the quiet patience of the stars.

He is so interwoven into nations,
Tangled with intrigue and false counter-schemes,
That he forgets these watchers at their stations
Where Space, for aeon on aeon, outstreams.

He has forgotten the single heart, the one
And unimpeded purpose of the soul;
The love that rises like the morning sun,
And sets upon a life made whole.

While you lay sleeping,
Floating on bracken-foam,
I sat listening,
Listening to the gentle fall of the beech-waves,
The green billows of leaves rolling on air.
'What ocean is this?' I wondered.
Though there was no reply, I knew
The meaning of this invisible indolence,
The wideness, the open light, the shade
Rolling on shade into green recess.
For threading the broad and spacious tide
Was glitter of wings vibrating
With shrill dart and venomous hum.
I knew too the pounding of blood,
The sullen flush in your face as you slept;
The energy burning my brain with a proud ambition
To be up, to be fathering life, and a thousand schemes,
Changing, and building; smashing my way through the tide.

Summer Night Music

Though the night was heavy, you should have stayed to hear
Music descending over the dark heat.
Day had been weary with sunlight, dust, and sweat;
But at the coming of night, there hovered near
A shadow like the antidote of fear;
Sound cool as any waters you could meet
In some green forest-basin, where the feet
Of deer have prinked a pattern year by year.

You lost that crystalline discovery,
That rock-cupped music falling on the dusk,
With briar, and nightstock, and contralto laughter,
And grateful whispering with breath of musk
When, the music ceasing, a moment after
A giant moon came gliding up the sky.

Tidings

Invisible, the messenger
Came and whispered close to her.
None saw her lean and tremble near;
None saw the passing cloud of fear
Across the sunshine of her speech.
Of what they murmured, each to each,
None of the friends assembled round
Heard or suspected any sound.
She did not even break the thread
Of skilful words with which she led
The weaving of that intercourse.
Yet through her lazy heart and brain
Which in this social ease had lain
Too long to bring her any rest,
There rushed a tide that stormed her breast;
Tumultuous news came flooding whence
The ocean of intelligence
Roamed unfathomably deep
Around the scattered isles of sleep,
Reached the white continent of thought
And round its broken bastions wrought
Thunder! She heard that music now:
Leaned, listened with hand-shaded brow,
Though wondering madly if she dare
Kiss the salt-encrusted hair
Of this traveller who came
Whispering, to her secret shame,
Pre-natal knowledge, with the sound
Of that tidal rhythm bound,
Bidding her womb grow reconciled
To tidings of an unborn child.

The Winter Students

You who are hidden away
Under the roofs of thought,
Forget that winter is gay,
Forget that the snow has wrought

A song unruffled by care,
Lighter than infant's breath
Caressing the sleeping hair;
A song that is smoother than death.

The Vagrant Scholar

The golden sunshine crept upon my book
And changed the pages to diminishing fields,
The words to bushes where the thrushes sang.
I wandered back where I had been before,
Page after page, enchanted with the grass,
The flowering hedgerow and the scented branch,
The rills with voice of linnets, and the birds
With music as of hidden waters tumbling
Through stones and mosses into secret pools.
I looked upon the wisest words again
And saw the sowers at their ancient work
Along the furrows gleaming through the clay.
The seed of thought, and seed for human bread,
Eternal beauty and immediate need,
Were scattered there before my hungry eyes
In that inspired confusion of the sun.

The Waterfall

All that long summer day the waterfall
Sang in the valley through the sullen wood,
And even the silent spaces where we stood
Were haunted with that low, leaf-hidden call.
We had to go, we had to leave it all,
The dome of air, the unimpeded flood
Of light, that lifted us, and fired our blood
To bird-flight up and over the mountains tall.

We had to fold our eagle-wings, and creep
Down through the sloping forest to the stream,
Down through the grotto-shades and dripping leaves,
Until we came where waters in their sleep
Were turning to the music of their dream,
Tossing white arms out of their scattered sleeves.

SCHERZO

Piccadilly Pastoral

Walking along the pavements in the rain,
I thought of summer, and the ripened grain
Rolling its golden billows in the lowland valley.
I heard above the dun rain and the din,
Lazy yellowhammers in the whin.
And I snuffed the scent of apples in the wet brick alley.

Yes, I saw 'buses come ambling down the hill
Coming to be milked at the call of Jane and Jill.
And the rabbits in the Circus where the hollow theatres stand
Were hurrying and scurrying across the thistled land.
Brown bracken, whose salt scent is borrowed from the sea,
Sighed with the passing traffic, and swung the resting bee.
Mingled with the uproar of the motor-vans and taxis,
I heard the falling timber, and the crash of woodmen's axes;
While basking on the green leaves of the Piccadilly clubs,
Fed greedy caterpillars, and fat and shining grubs.

Robin

One chill October morning
When day broke white and wan,
I heard a robin chitter.
The cheery little man!

'Cheep!   Cheep!
What shall I do with it?
Cheep!   Cheep!
Whatever shall I do with it?
Cheep!   Chirrup!   Cheep!
There's nothing to be done
With my old red waistcoat now I've a new one.'

Beech trees were beacons burning
Above the swaying mist,
Chestnut pods were falling
And their brown nestlings lost.

The elms, still proud with summer,
Yet in their windward tops
Hung the pale signs of ruin,
Like fever-stricken ships.

And to this world of wreckage
Lit by a ghostly sun,
The robin piped his worry
In wistful voice and thin.

'Cheep! Cheep!
What shall I do with it?
Cheep! Cheep!
Whatever shall I do with it?
Cheep! Chirrup! Cheep!
Oh, there's nothing to be done
With my old red waistcoat now I've a new one.'

The Valley by Moonlight

'Pass them on,' said the night priest,
Handing starry candles.
And the junipers
Twinkled with lights.
Distant hills too,
Floating on the billows of moonshine,
Bobbed their lanterns,
And the town below
Rode at anchor.

On Hearing the First Cuckoo

Oh Menelaus,
Oh my poor friend,
You have heard the news?
I know! I know!   They all betray us.
Sooner or later there comes an end
To kindness; and the winds of abuse
Nip the bud, shrivel the bloom.
Then marriage, with the promise of the bed,
Is a disgusting memory of betrayal,
Shame in the heart for words once said
With a bride now clasped to another groom.
Not the flesh, but the mind, Menelaus, is frail.

An Encounter

Stopping the Carmelite, I said,
'Father, do you know my joy;
Does your wisdom tell you why
I touch you in this traffic-din,
And lean toward your shaven head
And shout as though I were a boy
Brimming with lust of piracy;
Bursting with westward-bulging sails
Along the line to Barbadoes,
Riding Imagination's gales?'

The Carmelite shook his shrunken head,
Thrust out his heavy underlip,
And scratched his chin all razor-red.
'Of course I don't,' his solemn voice
With grim authority replied.
'Now were it lonely discipline
And sober thought made you rejoice,
And could I think the soul within
Was searching through your heart for sin,
Then . . .   Then . . .!'

                      I watched his beak
Thrust like an eagle at my face.
His voice rose to a parrot-shriek;
I trembled in that populous place,
Alone, alone, convicted then
Amidst my erstwhile fellow-men.
Then suddenly I saw his eyes
Shrinking with laughter, black and wild.
A red bandana bound his head;
His cutlass of a cruel size
Was spitted through a native child.
O then I understood his lies,
And loved the priestly things he said!

The Mouse

So still was the night,
So calm the pillowed world,
Even I might sleep,
Fall to oblivion,
Forget the goading brain,
The tyranny of thought.

Even I might sleep
Were it not for the sharp-eyed mouse,
The cruelty meek and small,
Crunching the boards beneath my bed.

The Sunset

It would be good, now,
To leap upon a horse,
And ride like a fond, romantic fool,
Into the sunset where the kings carouse,
Clinking their cups to fabulous women's eyes,
Their swords thrown steaming on the blood-red skies.
For reason at its best is a sorry tool;
My fingers tire of it.   For better or worse
I would clutch something sharper; knit my brows
On some insaner problem of the soul,
That has no answer hitherside the moon.

Oh moral priest; Oh counter-out of tills,
Have you not sometimes longed
To seek the Whore of Babylon, and croon
A lovesong in her bosom; then ride on
To hell, and snatch Boccaccio's quills
To write some pleasantry against the dead,
Till all the way to Paradise is thronged
With crowds of wanton laughter?

                              So have I done,
Rebel of virtue for fair virtue's sake,
Striving to put my handprint on the sun,
That I may touch the splendour, and awake
From righteousness, and find an empire won,
A kingdom of sufficient enterprise
To keep the music and its makers fed
Until the maddening sunset leaves the skies,
And we are citizens again,
Creeping upon the plain,
Moral, benign, with souls quite safely dead.

They might have taken sleep to be their god;
Crept to the arbour and the scented couch
With offerings to wealth.
                              But they were strong;
Strong with the single madness of the brain
That looks to innocence and childhood thoughts,
To the companionship of tinsel kings,
Outcasts, and ministers of fairy states,
The people of their early world.   They turned,
Walked backward through the present time,
Mad . . . mad . . . conjuring the past
With all its army of defeated pride.

The trampling of those feet, the cries and laughter,
Rose up like buffets of a southern gale
Upon an icebound world.   The summoners,
The fools, the innocents, suddenly turned,
Pointed to their monomaniac goal
And cried,
              'Here is our childhood host!   Stand back,
You cautious ministers, wielders of power,
You subtle-minded doctors of the State;
Here is an army that you cannot buy;
Here are the kings that journeyed from the East,
And all the crucified and laughing paupers.
We come to sweep ambitions, duty, fame,
Into a heap of autumn leaves, and fan
The flame with laughter, fire the rustling world
With laughter, until your craven citizens
Throw off their sleep, and dance about the pyre.
For we are mad, and young, and innocent.'

The Mistake

I read the name upon a tomb
Of a living man I know.
Was it some grim jest of doom?
Was it true, I cried?
                      Ah no!
For in flesh beside me there
Stood the victim of the jest,
Though his chattering teeth were bare,
And he clutched his bony breast,
Trembling lest that wild heartbeat
Might be only counterfeit.

Violation

I should have thought
This sanctitude might hush
That blatant-throated thrush.
But no!   The melancholy,
The green cathedral nave,
Turf-carpets quiet and holy,
Pregnant as the grave
Which is the womb of silence;
These fanes of thought were broken
Into with jubilance,
Shouts of indifference, jocund.
Jollyings, brave
Carousal and jest
From that drunkard
With the mottled vest.
Who filled his tankard?

The Carillon

At the ringing of the first bell,
Solitude, asleep in the Square,
Woke, cringing from the crowded air;
Saw the grinning echoes swell
And multiply, gesticulate and shout,
Till all the votaries of silence shrank
Into a stony semblance of rest;
Furry belly, feathered breast,
Into the warm dust pressed
For a moment of cacophonous terror,
Ere they scuttled and fluttered out,
Leaving their place to the clapper and throat,
The tumultuous dancing and riot
Advancing with bombast and threat
And as suddenly beating retreat.

Then to the violated Square
Solitude returned; gazed in the mirror
Of the fountain, dressed her dishevelled hair
With trembling hands, and stooped, and drank.

After the sun had sunk we lit the bonfire.
Day was fading in the clear delight
Of saintly sleep, closing her eyelids over
The iris of the heavens, brooding deep.
There was no taint upon the shrinking hills,
That shone so faint, as music soon to fade
Above the clear-plucked wires of harpsichords.
The silhouette of a nest with its tangled lace
Stood in a twig-bare tree against the sky.
Enboughed above it glowed two choral birds,
Hymning the grace of evening, joyful, loud.
The vesper star distilled her tears of light,
And the Hunter glittered bright, and fierce, and far.

Then we turned, and stooped, and lit the bonfire.

Slowly a little musing wisp of thread
Was twisted and drawn up from the mound
By some invisible hand overhead.   Grey,
Unbroken, untouched by the air, unfanned
By the wind, it rose with a gentle cobra-sway,
Swinging in some faint tide of the ethereal sea
Which sense feels not; which the spirit knows must be,
Since the soul with its hope in the same tide-rhythm flows.

Slowly the frail thread thickened into rope;
Still drawn up by the Unseen overhead;
Silken, and quickened to silver from the white
First pallid aftermath of light.
                            No sound
Came from the trees.   The thrush in her own song-trance
Was bound, and hushed into silence.
                                    Then a breeze
Came seeking the tomb of the day, to lay its sad
Tribute of perfume, holy breath of the mould.

Still for a moment the column of smoke unrolled.
Then the trees murmured, and in the mound beneath
The Demon of Fire turned, heard the sighing again,
With sudden scream of pain leaped up and burst
Through the piled sods of the wild Ætnean mound!

With eyes aghast we looked around on a world accursed;
On a tumid sky and the livid and leering forms
Of shadowy hordes that struggled, advanced, withdrew,
Hovered unseen, then leaped on the earth we knew,
Engulfed it, dwarfed it in the tumulous caverns of hell.
Darkness fell; but not on that Walpurgis ground.
Silence fell; but there no consecrated couch it found.
For from this running wound in the breast of night,
The slouching demons of fire, with shout, with torch,
Streamed out, and Earth was a place abhorred,
A midnight continent dreamed by the sick, insane,
And fever-goaded brain that dare not die.
Above, in the sky, the Savonarola-born
Billows of smoking blood-fire writhed and rolled.

As though to mock this traversty of morn,
A cock crowed thrice; and in our hearts there bowed
The faint-heart Peter, who had denied the Lord,
The reticent Glory, the Evensong of the bird.
Before His smoke-veiled throne we stood afraid.

Solace

It was not Father Time,
Nor the grim spectre of Death,
But a gentle old man
With asthma-dragging breath.

He was sweeping the leaves,
Clearing the heavy ground,
Raking them slowly,
Slowly into a mound.

Age-saddened and patient,
Smiling he said,
'They smell sweet as incense,'
And burned his dead.

The Ship

They have launched the little ship,
    She is riding by the quay.
Like a young doe to the river,
    She has trembled to the sea.

Her sails are shaken loose;
    They flutter in the wind.
The cat's-paws ripple round her
    And the gulls scream behind.

The rope is cast, she moves
    Daintily out and south,
Where the snarling ocean waits her
    With tiger-foaming mouth.

In April

My wits are not enough
To take this evening flame
And forge in it the stuff
Of song without a name,
An April lyric clean
As the orchard grass is green,
Shining as the bright
April evening light.
I have not yet lived long
Enough to be so young
As the old innocence
Of the eternal Spring.

Valour

Look at that mighty rook
Struggling against the morning sun—
See!   He is carrying a sword
Thrust out before him,
A flashing beak.

But the sun only laughs;
And playfully,
Absent-mindedly,
Trails the warrior's shadow
Through the grass and the primroses.

The Scout

Down came the horseman
Through the silent wood,
Like a tide of light,
Like an ocean flood.

Conies and foxes,
Every wildwood thing
Crouching in fright,
Heard the hard hooves ring.

Clean as a meteor,
Sharp as folding flame,
He circled and vanished
Swift as he came.

PENSEROSO

The Glance Backward

The dying beauty and the proud ascension!
Hark!   Hark!   What human story changes
In the far air of spirit, gathers cloudwise
And drops in rain of sound, sound purposeful,
Shapely, by the will of craft fashioned
At its outpouring into forms of memory,
Ancient and long-known forms of innocence,
Music some mother-voice once crooned, when, cradled
At breast, we looked up to the wing-filled heaven
And saw the bearded God pass staff in hand,
Brooding, wise, paternal, friend of childhood;
Pass by the weeping mother, while she hugged us
Deep to her breast?
                 The music fades, rises,
Thin as light, and piercing-quiet as morning,
With the retreating stars in anguish of eclipse,
Keener and fiercer as they pulse, extinguished
By day, sunrise, manhood, toil and din of traffic,
And the deathward swoon of the protective bosom
Leaving the hungry mouth adult and eager
To noontide sustenance of dust!
                      Oh, music!
Stream of paradisal milk, sustaining
The night of time, the garden-birth of mankind,
We hunger, we thirst, we are motherless, being rivals
Of God; Prometheans, demons, something more than mortal,
Surrendering the breast for prophecy,
Burying our mother and our little selves
Beneath our pride and childhood's fallen foliage.
We have set out upon the noon of triumph,
But in our dust that banished music tortures,
Mocks our male mouths that bleed with broken words.

The Response to Kings

Sometimes I think that if a certain king
Should come to my frail lodging on the world
And offer place and power, I should turn,
Confronting him with my ambition furled,
And broken pride trailed like a plover's wing.

For I am weary of the race; I burn
No more; I give no flame unto the winds'
Conflict.   Mine are other riches; hooded
Treasures of intimate thought; shaded glances
And subtle kisses with one whom the world finds
Not; one who has come with laughter, flooded
The tragic need, the tense and arrogant
Desire for mastery, the craving for acclaim.

With this companion I am greater than kings;
Content to take what comes from treacherous chances.
O King, however world-wide your renown,
I turn you from my door, with the proud things
That follow in the glory of your name.
For with my secret love I shall not want
Your panoply and strength, your proffered crown!

The Creation

Ah!   Let me close my eyes on this.
What I beheld shall thus remain
Recorded lifelong on my brain;
A scene of mingled hurt and bliss,
A sculptured and arrested strife,
A still epitome of life.

This shall become, as time wears on,
A legendary thing, that bears
An immortality of tears;
A joy mankind shall feed upon
When we, our matrix-moment past,
Have crumbled from this perfect cast.

Widow's Song

I thought it was the voice of my lover,
The cry of a voice long stilled:
But it was only a mourning plover
Wailing over the ploughed field.

O fiction of clod and furrow,
O naked pain of the earth,
I know you will haunt me to-morrow
With your skull-bare scream of mirth.

The Trees

All is quiet, and we wait
For the blossom-time of fate,
For the deep-implanted seed
To swell, to burst, to break the dome
Of the sleepy Earth, its home,
For our hunger is a greed
Not to be appeased by slumber;
Brain and heart have slept too long;
We must move to magic number,
Swing the sacred axe of song,
Fell the moaning trees that wake
Necromancy, evil spell,
Incantations o'er the bed,
O'er the tomb where we have slept
Uncomplaining, uninspired,
With the horizontal dead.

Time is lost, for Time has crept
With relentless subtle tread
On its mission overhead
While our maiden trance we kept.
Now we wake, and now we learn
It was Time that moved above.
We have slain the harmless trees.
They stood over us to mourn
Our sleep and slow oblivion.
Now we learn it was not these;
It was Time, that arid wind,
Silting death on dusty death
With its Earth-whirled orient breath.
Silent lay we there beneath,
Out of flesh and out of mind.

Music Recalled

Now that her music is silent
And sunk in the stream of years,
I find, in the murmur of viols,
A beauty and burden of tears,
A joy remembered in sorrow,
A passion of youth fallen cold,
A yesterday haunting to-morrow,
And a child grown knavish and old.

Waiting

They have done preparing now
For a guest they do not know,
For a little prince to come
To their hushed, expectant home.
Now their hearts and lips are dumb;
They are near the open door
Gazing out into the snow.
They can hear the spirit blow
Through the bushes, back and forth.
Is it happiness or woe,
Does it whisper death or birth?

The Wanderer

Your simplicity of heart;
The open candour of your mind:
Though I search through every part
Of the worlds of thought and sense,
Where shall I such freedom find
Though lifelong I wander hence
Through the jungle of my being
Where the sensual tigers tread
Tirelessly behind the fleeing
Deer of gentleness, until
Outworn, they tumble dead,
And the tigers take their fill;
Though I cross the desert then
Of my unknown fellowmen,
Finding sphinx and pyramid
Where their cryptic thoughts are hid,
Arid and unanswerable
Till the mind's divisions fall,
And united knowledge leaps
Impersonal to apocalypse?

Though these void adventures take me
In the treachery of unrest
From the home that you would make me
In the shelter of your breast,
I shall come again and find
Your old simplicity of heart
And the deep wisdom of your mind,
Nor a second time depart.

Museum Piece

That afternoon in the Museum
I felt my spirit die from the present,
Slip from the clasp of loved hand
And touch the dust of a lost land.
There I met a Saxon child,
Upon her finger-bones a ring
Whose gold was faded, as in Spring
Rainwashed primroses shine.
A little garnet blind with time
Was set within it, shared the sleep
Of milkwhite skin and August hair,
That hair of autumn wheat, with deep
Sunflecks, and the windy shadows
Kissing the gold, and settling there
Like happy thoughts on innocence.

But now the garnet glowed, the gold
Clung to the living flesh that gleamed
And pulsed as the blood flowed beneath.
From the awakened eyes there streamed
The light of mind: and I heard breath
Make music in her mouth, not old
Harsh rustling from the grave of thought,
But tenderness, sweet enquiry,
Quick with suspense, rapid with running
After life, after colour, tasting these
With timid, child-bold ecstasies.

It was a voice I knew, calling
'Father! Father!' in the Saxon speech;
Falling on my heart, falling
From a century where I could not reach,
Shouting over her shoulder as she ran,
'I have left a message!   Make haste!
Follow me, Father!   Follow!   Follow!'

Striving after her, to come to her side
And clasp my darling, my spirit died.
Echoed in my ears 'Make haste!   Make haste!'
And the faith of that eager 'Follow! Follow!'
Then the dust of the Museum settled low,
The dust of time and human waste,
And I said, my voice drawn thin and hollow,
Said to my loved one, 'Shall we go?'

Lunatic

As I looked up the steep hillside
To the beechwood comb along the ridge,
I saw the rich full moon upride
Above the branching prongs.   Her edge
Was brittle with the fingering frost.
The air was broken too; it cut
My eyes, until the sight was lost—
The ridge, the wood, the lonely hut,
The moving sheep beneath the moon,
The little coil of cottage smoke!
Even the vision in my mind
Of someone waiting there within—
I lost that too; it lay behind
These knives of night, fine-tempered, thin;
Behind their lifted blades, steel-blue,
That stabbed, and stabbed with icy stroke,
Freezing me inward, till I stood
A statue in moonlight, blotting some stars,
Timeless, chipped with cosmic scars,
And fabulous to human blood.

A Letter

To-day I had a letter
From a boy seeking fame.
How ingenuous he was,
How clumsy and arrogant,
Talking about himself
In the same old, stale way,
Blinded by the same old fantasies,
Lured by the mirage of ignorance.

But as I read,
Blushing for him,
My heart sank:
Despair swept over me
Like wind through a leafless tree;
And I trembled with shame
For my emptiness,
For my greedy envy
Of this foolish prince.

The Mountain

Though it was noonday, and high summer,
With tolerant warmth roaming through the town,
Our hands, in touching, touched a ghost.
Quickly we looked, to see if each had heard,
Above the indolent passing of the crowd,
That faint bell, ringing in the pass
Over the cloud and snowy precipice.

Both heard it; both saw the mountain,
Distant, and calm, and terrible as death.
We heard the music of the cataract
That tumbled in the ravine, mumbling
Through its white beard, blind and mad.
We saw the fatal ridge, the trickling
Stain of crimson creeping to the flowers
That dropped their perfume on the upturned face.
And the impassive silence of the pines,
The cold sentinels against the sky,
Enfolded us below the cruel peak,
Denying the madness of the falling water,
Denying the broken body fallen on flowers.

Oh, we shall haunt for ever that mountain place.
That poisonous loveliness has frozen for ever
Summer and city pleasure out of our hearts.

Reproach

Oh you who should be sleeping in the grave,
Pillowed on gold, the treasure of your beauty,
Can you not be content with what you have?
Must you draw down, and hold beside you there,
My thought, my lingering vitality,
That still supports me in this solitude,
Feeding me with the sparse crust of regret
And the thin wine of memory?   You covet this,
You raise your unforgettable hands out of the grave
And rob me of my ease in poverty,
Taking my last and only sustenance.
Oh, I am hungry here, because of your greed.

Sleep

We were so weary underneath the trees.
The music drifting from the orchestra, flowing
Slowly on, would pause, and dip, and stop,
Baffled by clouds of sleep floating across
Our minds, looming shapes barring the way.
Green billow on billow above our heads
Rising and falling and rolling with foam of leaves
Into the beam of the lamps where trafficking moths
Fluttered and touched in dusky thoroughfare;
These we watched, lost, and found again
As the clouds, carved with towers of dream,
Galleoned over us, fantasy shouldering real.

Who were you, in that island of sound and sleep,
Earth drooping beneath you, a wide sky
Furling its wings and unfurling them over your beauty;
Were you that woman whom at first meeting I loved,
Suffered for, fought for, centre of all my hope;
You, now fading before me, your hand a ghost,
Your breast shrunken, your lids fallen, your voice vanished?

Ah this warm drug of sleep, veiling our faith;
Cloaking our worship, our love, and our ancient thought
With fog that follows the stream of our tropical blood;
Where is the fount of this river we cannot ford?

Betrayal

Betrayed by the flood
The house stood deserted.
The walled-in waters prowled
From room to room,
Dark and smooth.
And blindly following them
Bobbed a drowned doll.

Among the refugees
One little face
Glowered tragic and resentful,
Dumbly hating the elders
Who could not understand,
Who would not go back.

From an Upland Valley

In a high valley of the hills
Where the wind spun Earth
In a gust of mirth,
I saw the conflict of our wills:
You the wild
Unreconciled
Self-diviner, trustless, true
Only to the cruel self in you;
Cruel yet kind,
Harsh, tortured mind,
Worse than wanton, sweeter than faith;
I saw you, heard you, fought you—wraith!

There is no absence now you have come
Into this vale we call
Life, where the winds fall
Like eagles on quarry, thrusting home,
Then lulling to dear
Confidences, near
Whisperings, close, so intimate
There's hardly room for love or hate
To slip between.
For what has been,
Was past, is present, will future be,
One piercing agony, one joy for me.

And you, so swift, so sure, burnt clean
And sparse with your soul-inflicted pain,
What have you left to feel?
Could you see the trees kneel
As they kneel here beneath the storm,
Bowed with invisible alarm
Down to stones, grasses,
Sheep-runs, hare-passes,
Shuddering under the siffling wrath
That hisses through each gap and path;
Could you be near me
Would your mind sear me,
With such a wild exemplar by
As this embrace of earth and sky?

I torture you, I who am still
Yours, shall be till death takes his fill
Of the brimmed lake
Whereat we slake

Our thirst, self poured on self, and run
Into such stillness under the sun
That light is pain,
And loss is gain
Refracted from that source of pleasure.
Oh, brood on this, dear heart, at leisure;
Absent, here,
Gone, but near,
Your passion is flame you cannot measure!

The Call

Strange, that a barn, and a cow
Knee-deep in nettle-foam,
Should call my ambitious thoughts
So quietly home:
Bow down my brain under dreams
Of simple troubles, and themes
Built of tragical memories of youth
Whispering close, like truth,
Like childhood, 'Come!
My little one; poor, dumb
Little one, seeking your home!'

The Return to the Orchard

Overblown with seeding grass
The old orchard was:
The brickpath and ashpath
Laid but a year,
Now hidden. Creeping near,
I saw no feet had trodden
There. They were rain-sodden.
Great hemlocks, and sorrel
With fingers of coral
Moved with the breeze
Under the bearded trees.
No birds were singing;
No children swinging.
I wondered, calling,
'Hallo! Hallo! I've come!'
But no little ones ran out
With welcome and boisterous shout.
Only the ancient trees
Stood secret and dumb.

The Travellers

We had forgotten, she and I,
My generous friend of four years old,
How far it was toward the sun.
Our hands were idle with the cold.

She had stopped still beneath a yew
Where cruel spines lay for her tread,
A solemn tree, with poison-drops.
She looked, and wondering, shook her head.

She was so weary with the road
That all her trust grew tired, and stared
Out of her eyes, and asked me 'Why?'
I should have answered had I dared.

I, who had mastered many things,
Wiseacre of my span of years,
Knelt down, thrice-humbled, to confess
Before the knowledge in her tears.

The Storm-cock

Why should you trouble me thus
With the accusing future,
The magnificent deed to be done,
Oh prophet of brown feather,
Shouting into the sun
From the elm tree's highest bough?

Look down upon me with pity.
I stand with the irons of the past,
The fetters of conscience and duty,
Clanking at ankle and wrist.
The clumsy god of my fathers
Deafens me, shatters my brain.
How can I heed you, divine
Prophet on wind-ruffled feathers?

Shall I be up and away
To a destiny once foretold
Before my fetters were forged?
What is the triumph you cry,
What passion gloriously urged,
What wonderful worship spilled
On a cold, indifferent sky?

PART SIX

NEWS FROM THE MOUNTAIN

1932

News from the Mountain

To you who creep below
Upon the ocean-bed of air,
I sound this trumpet-blare
From my island peak of snow.

With two companions shadowing my side
I climbed the foothills where the harvest hung
Flank-high in foaming blossom round the oxen;
Cushion and bell, spire and tumbled shock
Of perfume-dripping bloom.   Then I strode higher,
And from my right hand fell old comrade, Sorrow;
Turned back and sought the richer plains again,
To brood, and mourn the losses of the past,
Assessing death by the wealth of the summer world.

Then, with that other faithful by my side,
I left the upland meadows, the mellow tongues
Of cow-bells half confused with sleep and flowers.
The silence of the forest waited us.
I trod the carpets, century-deep and still,
My footfall noiseless as that dour companion
Who shadowed me in darkness.   So close he kept,
There was no need to whisper his command.
I had him in my heart.   Even the new
Authority of darkness under the pines
Could not envelop Memory.

                    We climbed
Together in the quiet, unhaunted wood,
Through silence, and the mist of under-boughs
Falling in umber veils.   Beyond the larches
We rose past boulders, gentian, coralline moss,
And touched the white paws of the mountain creature,
The first snow bedded in a breast of cowslips.
The padded claws dabbled in that fragrance.
Here we reached the roof of sober thought,
The ordered house of Man.   Beyond it lay
The white panther, indolent in the light,
Dreaming its lithe and beautiful desire,
Calm snow-death, and the cruelty of ice.

I thought that my companion would have urged
Comparison with the half-familiar valley
And the habitual plain: but when I turned,
No shadow lay at my left hand.   Memory was gone,
Had slunk into the forest aisles, to pace
The hushed cathedral carpet of the larches,
To brood, and count the follies of the past.

No shadow now to right or left, I climbed
Through the thin ether till I reached this place,
Thought's ocean surface, where the snowbergs float.
Here stand I careless of my lovely dead,
Those whom I mourned below.

                                    Cruel as stars,
And passionless as moonlight, I look down
Upon the waves of that mercurial sea
Which lies in lazy grandeur on human earth,
Where all I was, and ever might be, sleeps,
Sleeps on beneath the drug of material air.
Now without mercy, I wake to solitude,
Lift up the silver trumpet of my madness
And blow defiance over the huddled world.

The Mountain Lake

Empty of heart we wait amid the snow,
The feline snow that crouches by the lake.
Empty of heart, except for icy fear
Reflected from unfathomable deeps,
Blue beyond blue, past the inverted pines,
Past mirrored fangs laid bare against the sky,
Past silent air, and silence in the vault,
The iris of the mountain, hiding thought
No human fear might hide, or love reveal
Within the eye, lake of the human soul.

We know this presence.   From the valley first
Lifting our eyes toward the mountain wall
We saw the morning tremble in the deep
Where the night's constellations lay dissolved.
We saw the sun, with cautious sword out-thrust,
Creep with that misted blade from height to height,
Testing ravine and bastion and crag
With ringing blows of light.   The splintered gold
Broke gaily over forest, lanced the snow
And melted to the valley with delight.

That visible laughter made the earth respond.
An eagle first, immovable above
The highest reach of alp, fluttered its pinions
And then relapsed to stoniness in air.
Larks and cascades competed in their song,
Each conjuring, with throat and rock-foot pool,
A clamour of laughter such as silver takes
Webbed in a girl's gold hair when snaring with it
The first desire of boyhood.   From the slopes
Below the alpine panther's drooping pads,
The little cowslips ran like bees disturbed
By a marauding bear.   Innumerable flowers
Lifted their heads and flung toward the sun
Their tiny shouts of perfume, breaking together
And deluging the valley with the riot
Of morning-joy indistinguishable from mirth
Of mortal lips and innocence of meadows.

And through this gaiety we took our way
Against the onrush from the slopes above,
Pageant and cavalcade of song and colour,
Dancing and miming of the naked mists
Down through the boulder-rooted woods that stood
Aloof and stubborn, except for the young larches
Who trembled, sighed, and shook their verdant hair.

But all this masquerade from dawn to noon
Borne down against our ascent, could not blind
Our eyes, nor cover the knowledge in our hearts.
We saw, we knew the monster of the ice,
The glacier, the morain of the rocks,
The cleft concealed with a faint feather of snow,
The horror of the silence in the height
Turning to murmur of its own despair.
We knew that as we climbed we should encounter
This powdery spirit like the breath of fear,
Invisible, yet glinting in the air
Above the peak, and shaking through sunshafts
Its venom of resentment on the soul
Of man, of eagle, lark and wild cascade,
The little flowers shouting to the valley,
Frosting them all with leper-touch of terror
Colder than echo, quieter than death.

Summer Night

Night was slow in coming
As with eyes of middle-age
We gazed at the year's young page:
The foal at its mother nosing,
The marsh-flowers closing
Against a few bees humming;
A drunken thrush yet strong
In his braggart song;
A cuckoo elusive still
From an unexistent wood
Dreamed of behind the hill
At whose dark base we stood
Both sleepy with the sun,
Yawning for night to fall,
And the cuckoo's last clear call,
That lingering one
Which dies and is blent
From sound into scent
Of beanfield and white
Sensual body of night.

The Sound Within

Without misgiving, to be lost
A mile above the plain,
Enveloped in a mountain mist,
And the day dying.

Each berry of the rowan tree
With ghostly globe attached;
Strange binaries to greet the eye
As the night approached.

Soundless, sightless, in the height,
Creatures of space we stood,
Defiant of the drums of fate
Patrolling through our blood.

The Parallel

He was begotten by God alone!
The story is well known,
With legend of a tower of gold,
A maiden therein who enticed
The morning to her breast,
And by this passion from the East
Mothered a little Perseus Christ.

His boyhood was remote and strange;
With flight before an elder's wrath,
By sand and ocean-wave to range,
Winding a devious path.
Lost to mankind for sake of man
He moved protected by the Lord.
Wisdom before him ran
With a mirror; Hermes with a sword.
Fisherfolk befriended him,
To guide, and follow where he came
Upon the Gorgon lying grim
Along the Temple porch, where wrote
Money-changers without shame,
Who bartered innocent blood
For mysteries once understood.

To cleave the Beast through flesh and bone,
Change theologians to stone,
He raised the mirror, gazed therein,
Lifted the sword, and smote!
Thereafter went he through the Earth,
To Heaven by way of Hell;
The triumph of a virgin birth,
As God and womankind know well.

The Prison

No sound!   No sound!   But far away
    The murmur of mankind,
And near at hand the grating lock
    That turns upon my mind:

That turns upon the summers gone,
    And sets the seal of pain
Before the loved, unhappy dead
    Imprisoned in my brain.

One leaden eve, returning
  At melancholy pace,
My dark thoughts inward burning
  Upon the heart's disgrace,

I saw the sunset leering
  With one satiric beam,
As though the gods were jeering
  At my unfruitful dream.

Impersonal, sardonic,
  It closed the wasted day,
A shrewd and bitter tonic
  To brace me on my way.

Challenge to Dualism

Day comes again to Earth; she rolls
Love-drowsy, shuddering to her lord
Who shakes with his triumphant mirth,
Clean, and empty of desire.

Slowly she wakes, remembers, flushes
With thought of midnight, lifts her voice,
Until the sky is mad with lark-song,
The valleys with the clarion cock,
The woods with ousel-flute, triple
Shout of thrush, and chorus of finches.

Who could conceive such purity
Rose from the sweet exhaustion of love;
Dew from abandonment, with gold
Of dust-mote morning, daffodil
Mood, and music of the brooks;
Emblems of our Mother's lust
When she lay shadowed under the Sun
And took his fire into her womb?

A Procession

Marvellous wings filled the morning:
The bourdon bee from grass
To grass heaved his brown sacks;
The butterfly battled with air,
Adorning her wings with light.
Beetles with armoured backs
Flashed steel and bronze so bright
That a king, it seemed, must pass
For the hordes of the orchard to stare,
Raise huzzah and buzz
With rustic gossamer wing,
Their acclamation thus
Catching sunshine, noon-sound,
Hay-height above the ground,
Though none quite glimpsed the king.

Crevasse

For those in peril on the deep!
But what of this, the narrow ledge,
The rope that chafes and strands
Upon the flaw's ice-tempered edge
As one by one the climbers creep
With death at feet and hands?

Where the rock looms, a little cave
Affords a shelter that is false.
There fear can halt, and hear the pulse
Of the rebellious heart-beats crave
Rest from the climbers' will.

One waits within that grim panache:
The other clambers still
Higher, hacking niche by niche,
Seeking slowly to escape
As wrecked mariners grope
Shoreward to the sky,
Upward to the light.

Above him looms the jagged scarp.
A thousand feet below him lie
The mastered moments of the fight.
With threat above, and threat below,
He cuts, and calculates the leap,
Knowing his comrade does not know
The treachery of the glacier-steep.
An instant's pause to test the rope;
Then, linking skill with desperate hope,
He jumps!
        The other hears a cry,
And turns to see a shadow run
Across the cavern floor and fly
Over the vault and out to follow
The rope that races past and snaps!

If he leans thus, he 'll see perhaps
That which he dreads to see.   He calls!
And echo answers hollow
From scarp, and glacier-bed, and walls
Now graceful with the evening sun.
But there is no reply.

In the Beginning

One night, in a silent world,
The book upon my kneebones chafed:
And as I turned the page, my hand
Withered, shed its flesh, and rattled
From period to period, bone by bone.
Even my brain lost animal warmth,
Nor grew with leaves of tree-like thought.
Back to the skeleton and rock
I sank, reversal of a moon,
Dying to infancy again,
But not to the sweet childhood marrow.
Ah! Beyond that to the first
Congealing of the element,
Shrinkage of unnative ether
Into this temporary rock
Which Atlas for a moment holds.

So sat I for a star-life there,
The very self of firmaments;
Before all knowledge, younger than thought;
God's innocence, if God *was* then.

138

Two Men Dream a Dream

Maddening, to dream thrice of tonic air
Heavy in the lowlands, and find a stranger there
Corroborate the dream, confirm the scene,
The mood, the moment, shouting aloud, 'We 've been!'
And fill the glass with gold, and drink again
To that unreal adventure from the plain
With only fantasy for guide, when day
At midnight broke upon our sleep through grey
Mists of the brain!
           Unsubstantial stuff
For a shy Englishman who had seen enough
Of pain too private, and politics too wide,
To range abroad and share with a dark-eyed
Levantine, who no doubt would show his grief
To half the world, but keep his comments brief
When any vague idealist from the north
Should indiscreetly seek to draw him forth
On questions of his country's politics.

A pleasing whim of destiny to fix
On such unlikely fellows to combine
At their first meeting, over southern wine,
In the sharp exultation of a dream;
Each with the other sharing the wild gleam
Of recognition, confirming it with shy
Incredulities of eye to eye.
We told of our adventure in the night,
The setting forth together by the light
Breaking from the impossible east of the mind.
We shared the same first murmur of the wind
As dawn's hand touched the pines, and made them call
—Raising their sleeves of snow, letting them fall—
A secret world-disturbing plaint, half sigh,
Half silence.   We looked together at the sky
For signs of warning, such as mountaineers
Take with that sixth sense born of vanished fears
And old disastrous moments.   And we saw
No writing thereon of the alpine law
Forbidding us the glacier, the fang
Thrust through the snow, as though death's challenge rang
Over the seductive purity of height
Beyond his herald eagle's boldest flight,

And froze his horrid voice to rocky scarp
For ever visible, both shrill and sharp
Together, disharmony of sight and sound,
Presiding grimly over level ground!

Before the wine was finished we had scaled
—Safe in the café garden, as day failed
And flushed the mountains with a lingering glance—
The foothill, the first forest-belt, the chance
Panther-foot of snow bedded on soft
Cushions of pines uprooted from aloft
And piled like feathers underneath that paw
Of feline softness.
               Having crossed that flaw
In the serenity of nature's love,
We braced ourselves for tougher work above,
And with that task surmounted, set ourselves right
For the less playful humours of the fight,
Testing our ropes, our axes; giving shrewd
Taps to our determination; viewed
Our last three hours of ascent, and then plunged
Into the abysm of height, where silence lay
Deeper than in the long-deserted halls
Of old Atlantis, where even no fin calls,
No nautilus, or wandering life of lace,
Ventures with trail of upper-ocean grace
Born of the murkiest filterings of light.

By now the café-terraces were bright
With twinkling lamps in the acacia boughs
And cruder beams escaping from the house.
The highest peak our dream had yet to climb
Rose up beyond the lake, remote, sublime.
Fading between the dayfall and the flood
Of a half-focused moon.
               The stranger stood,
Lifted his glass, and toasted the austere
And unattainable symbol of our fear;
Drank to that, and to the dream come true
Through being shared so madly by these two
Uncomprehending, incompatible,
Each feeling that the other called him fool!

'Well now?' he said; and waited my reply,
Distress unspoken glinting in his eye.
'What now?' I answered, staring through my wine
At the unmentioned summit whose divine
Countenance was whispering the moon
Secrets of pearl, as young Endymion
Once raised his pallid face beneath her dew
And learned to be a god.
                              'Shall we pursue
This tale of our coincidence, and go
Fulfil our dream, and prove it true with snow,
With desperate adventure, and perhaps—death?'

The raised glass trembled once.   I held my breath,
And watched the hand grow steady as he spoke.
'I did not reach the top,' he said.   'I woke!'

Then I, the Englishman, did not confess,
But turned aside to cover my distress,
And in so doing saw the mountain gleam
With distant scorn of my unfinished dream.
I sought to hide my shame; but for all I willed,
The Levantine remarked my wine was spilled!

Refutation

I crumble in my fingers
This handful of sweet mould.
How passionate its savour.
I breathe it, and inspire
The life inherent,
The violet-promise,
The prophecy of wheat.
Here is my substance,
My lasting life:
Here is my strength
To challenge Plato
Who denied his own mother
In this handful of earth.

The Solitary Climber

Dark engines of the blood
    That pound from birth to death,
I heard them as I stood
    With the wide earth beneath.

No other sound, no bird,
    No murmur in the grass,
No mountain-echoed word,
    Nor foot upon the pass.

Only the sullen roar
    About my brain and bone
While giant-like I bore
    The firmament alone.

A Vision of Battle

Swift to the command of sleep,
    My dream divided space and time:
I passed the herdsmen and their sheep
    On hillsides white with morning rime.

The southern passes through the snow,
    The glacier ravenous with death;
I breasted these, and saw below
    The valleys veiled in their own breath.

The centuries at my travelling fled,
    Their cruel laws for once repealed;
And from the ground uprose the dead,
    The Gipsy hosts on Mohac Field.

I saw the Crescent long abhorred
    By Kings of Christendom who raised
The Cross and Garment of the Lord,
    And yelled 'The Turk!   Now God be praised!'

A Night in Middle-life

At forty years we find the nightingale
Loses a little of her heart-throat song
That shakes the woodland, turning youthful lust
Into religion, cloister of the womb,
And monastery of lips.   Jasmine and whorl
Of drunkard woodbine made those nights divine,
Touching the senses which had never sipped
And drugging them to ineffectual madness.

Had then some maiden breast slipped like the moon
From vesture of a cloud . . . but thought was false,
Too solid in an unsubstantial world
Of innocence, yearning, mirages of youth.
The ripe grass, bowing laden to the moon;
The heavy moth, staggering with desire,
Falling from poppy into eglantine,
Both flight and destination drained of colour
In the cool passion of starlight, and the drift
Of northern fire between the short descent
Of summer day seeking another dawn;
These were enough for innocence to flush
Blood-filled with longing for it knew not what,
So long as God had lips, and Christ had limbs
To clasp and bear the virgin spirit down,
Ravish the maidenhead, and rising, leave
Or boy or girl in fruitful-wise, to grow
With this new seed of wisdom, passion-sown,
Slowly, with grief and shame, to adult strength,
And in maturity bring forth a child,
The very soul of love begot by God
Upon the innocence of morning worlds;
The fruit so feared by man that he contrived
To subjugate it once upon a cross,
And in hypocrisy kneel down to worship
The fragile virgin whom the God deflowered,
The maiden pregnant with the Crucified.

The Anchorite's Lament

Not utterly complete,
My solitude was sweet;
But now my dear companion
Must needs abandon
The friendship of our cave,
Preferring the small grave
My hands have dug him.
It was my last endeavour
For one who understood
My silence, every mood.
He now sleeps for ever.
Let the earth hug him!

At daybreak he would stroke
My laggard eyes, and wait
Till orisons were spoke.
Were I weary or late
How bravely would he scold,
Calling me sluggard, old
In sloth, self-pitiful.
I understood him well,
Though all the words he used
Were cries shrill and hoarse.
Yet kings have said worse,
And lovers bemused
Were less eloquent
Than my raven, chance-sent;
Poor broken-wing
Who lacked voice to sing.

His croaking would start
Tears in the desert,
Wake laughter among the rocks
Where I am condemned
By conscience to dwell,
With no womankind
To flatter me well,
Bid my soul take ease
And my brain to sleep;
Use treacheries
Of beauty; hair, lips, eyes,
And yielding flesh,
To plunge me deep
In kindness, and my soul enmesh.

No eremite before
Had such a monitor
So watchful and sombre
Over his sins.

By day, mine would slumber
Beneath his black cloak;
At dusk, with spread wings
He must chuckle and croak;
A fine fit to make me
My task forsake me
And turn to prayer.
He would ask, after,
His corn and water.
I gave him no flesh,
That he must seek alone
Out in the bush.
I would not traffic there,
Nor countenance his thirst
For meat, his one lust.

Alas, he 'll hunt no more,
Nor may I go railing
Against that carnal failing.
What virtuous airs he wore!

Now must I turn alone
To this lust of my own,
With none to compare it,
No fellow to share it.
Sin that lurks hidden
Yet gains no dominion,
By vigilance forbidden,
Makes a cruel companion.
But now 'tis all I have,
My sable crony gone
At last to his grave.
Thy Will be done.

The Eight Men

The tower is silent as we mount,
Except for the ancestral clock
Who clucks a little iron tongue
Each second of time, as he has done
For twenty generations to count
In drops of baptism, and the knock
Of earth on coffin, one by one—
Life unwinding, life outspun.

Shuffle of leather on the stone;
A feather-quilted bird who wakes
And shakes a wing, that makes alone
A little fury in the quill
And then subsides.   All is still.

Round by round, the belfry stair
Falls below us; through the slit
We see a winter world, moonlit;
Midnight roofs, trees black and bare,
A horse who breathes the silver air
Beside the graveyard wall.   And then
Eight friendly, local Englishmen,
All of one parish, doff their coats,
Set down the lantern by the wall,
Husk a few words, and clear their throats,
Unknot the snaky ropes, and stand
Each with a demon under his hand,
His iron slave poised for the fall.

There is no other sound at all:
The bird sleeps, the trees outside
Finger the stars, and catch the white
Frost-fallings of the Christmastide,
But make no movement: far and wide
The fields are frozen; the rusty vane
Groans; then the world is quiet again.
Only the clock: 'Tick! . . . tock! . . . *tack* . . . tock!'

'Ready?' says the tenor; but none replies.
We wait, we are ready; eight pairs of eyes
Glance swift answer; eight arms lift.
'Then . . . go!' he shouts, and one by one
The eight arms swing down, and down
Bang the bells!   The belfry holds
The fury, hollows itself and folds

146

The flood from clapper and rim, but soon
The tower is swimming, the octaves rise
On their own ringing selves and fling
Out and over the fields, the skies.
Even the silver frost, the hoar moon
Hum with their metal glint, the trees
Crook their fingers, pluck the stars
That ring out with their jewelled voices.
Hard echo upon salvo, back and forth
From High Piper to Tenor, mad Christian mirth
Half sinful with the pagan Earth,
Defying the silence of the spheres,
The frost, that ghost of Time, the fall
Of the eternal Light, all Powers unanswerable.

The old horse grazes by the churchyard wall.

The Midnight Motorists

Turning by the warren in the wood,
Cautious, peering through the streaming screen
Out on a vertical-flowing world, a flood
Falling, a fantasy by no man seen
Who has not looked through glass and been afraid;
Suddenly we saw a fire resist
The downward flow; a little flame that made
A marble's revolution, like a cist
Twirled sore upon the sable skin of night.
Steadfast upon its shining core it spun
Clockwise; paused; reversed; gaily spurning
The falling universe; a sister sun
In mocking parallel beside it burning.
How could we know, concerned for our souls' sake,
That to some cowering beast we were the Snake?

The Pagan

Once, on a burning August day
    Along the plain of France,
I saw beside the poplared way
    A gipsy maiden dance.

She had a hemlock in her hand,
    Her eyes were wild with wine;
And round her shoulders bare and tanned
    I saw a grass-snake twine.

Too often now, eyes closed in prayer
 Among my Christian kind,
I watch that serpent-goddess flare
 On the greensward of my mind.

Houses to Build

I hear men tell of another war
To wage where bramble blossoms star
The inverted firmament beneath
The pine trees and the silent heath.

It is a war of pick and hod,
For Lares, hearth and threshold god,
Fought with mortar, lime, and brick
Against the ancient ones who flick
Scut, flash feather or fin,
Sheathe claw, tread on thin
Pad, pry with whisker or beak;
All creatures piteous and meek.

I hear the death-knell of the fern;
I snuff the bracken-fires that turn
To furnace where the golden sap
From fallen pine-cone cap
Runs in oblation on the soil,
Sacred amber, holy oil,
Invoking vainly all the lost
Deities of the wildwood host:
Pixies, elves, the god of frogs
And quaking midgets of the bogs;
Dryads with their beech-bark skin;
All who pried upon the Sin
Which provoked our human need
For cloth to hide our loins' harsh greed;
For shelter under clannish tents
From light, and air, and innocence.

These were the naked loves who saw
Penates build the moral law,
Lay the hearth, set wall and roof
That fallen Man might draw aloof
From happy feather, fur, and fin,
To brood upon his branding Sin.

The Veteran

Long time ago it was that he set out
On that too-mortal journey to the grave.
Behold him now!   His hair, his shrivelling cheek,
That battered eagle-beak, the shadowed cave
Each side the neck, the bogle of the eye
Somewhat too creaking and too lustreless!

But are we fair?   We have perhaps observed
Nothing interior; the slim proportion
Of the prophetic spirit given him
When he set out.   Since then he's lived and loved
And lost and loved again, a life of pain
And fitful hope, and merit frittered away
In lust and whim, the habit of carnal dust.

But ask him, has he truly had his day?
He once began as boatman to a queen,
And took her on the midnight water, thrust
Music into her arms, called her 'Isolda'
Mightily, with opening manhood in his throat.
And it is said she leaned, unlaced herself,
Gave him her moonlit breasts, and set her mouth
Faithfully on his, with only the film between
Of the salt sea-tang.
                         But after that the tale
Grows dim with shame, humanity too frail
For such august companionship.   The helm slipped,
The ship subsided slyly upon the shallow,
And over the hidden sands a mocking laughter
Rang hollow, with the departure of the queen,
The boatman left to listen the demands
Of the low murmuring waters through the night;
Little wavelets, puritans of conscience,
Lapping the wreck-side round his solitude.

Do not believe that was the end.   He might,
With age-encrusted voice, sadly imbued
With wisdom savouring of the foxy grape,
Reply that then the true beginning dawned,
From doxy unto virtue, in the shape
And frugal flavour of a continence
Enjoined by fear and late humiliation.

'Twould save his pride, and make his evening sweet
With thoughts of some accomplishment at least
To furnish him with his own funeral feast.

But stand aside discreetly: look again
From this more sympathetic point, and watch
The slavering mouth ('twas there Isolda clung),
The swollen joints, the sharp asthmatic ratch
In the breast—but we will waive the rest,
And think on prudence that has come to this;
The puritan triumphant over thought
Of a queen wrecked, a promise thrown away,
And betrayal of the god behind the kiss.
Pity the virtuous picture time has wrought
Of one who dreams that he has had his day.

The Shop-girl

Facing the storm of the summer sale,
The shop-girl, once a healthy country lass,
Mouthed automatic phrases to the horde
Of bargain-ravenous women.
Wave after wave, scented, angry, and hot,
They rolled their airless breath over her breast.
Sometimes she swayed upon her aching legs,
While *Modom this* and *Modom that* she lisped
In large-store accents quite devoid of life.

But to herself she said soft, rustic words,
Rough fledglings in the nest, or cottage moths
That come to lamplight from the currant-beds.
She crooned them to her heart, and fostered them
With memories of dew and mushroom rings;
Clusters of hazel nuts just lover-high,
And berries even past reach of lover with girl
Kissed, and shouldered, and told to bend the bough.
And oh, the laughter, like a river gem;
The touching of lips as though they were birds' wings;
Sweetness in the grass; the giving with a sigh;
And to be there, with *him* so treacherous again . . .

But there's the shopwalker, pausing, and passing by,
'Yes, *modom*, quite *cherming*.   We also have it in plain.'

Compensation

Bright-eyed youngster, say,
If you can read the future,
Will you regret to-day,
The wild surprise of nature;
Bird-song, bloom, and rapture,
And lips you dare not capture
Yet soon will touch with your own
And find the secret flown?

I once was your age, truly
Bold and shy by turn.
I took my maiden duly,
And found still more to learn.
Soon gone was that sweet fooling;
Life brought a greyer schooling.
Yet since that harsh betrayal
Joy has not seemed so frail.

Reprieve

Ah God!   The joy to come
At length stumbling home!
After the frown, the curse,
The foreign hands, and worse,
The clang of iron on rock,
The shriek of key in lock,
The fetters in the hell
Of thought-infested cell!
And after sentence done,
To be thrust into the sun,
The long-forgotten light
In blind and cringing plight!
They did not know, who sneered
As drunkenly I veered,
That earth and sky so vast
Were swords I shuddered past:
They did not know I saw
The horror of the Law
Haunting the world of the free;
And so they stared at me
Until I felt the brand
Betrayed upon my hand.

Yes. As they looked and scoffed,
The garb but lately doffed
Still burned me to the bone.
But though I stood alone
Before mankind's derision
With the universe my prison,
I found by instinct there
The pathway to my lair,
The instinct of the brute
Bleeding, hunted, mute,
To join its mate: I found
My love, my holy ground.
Ah God, the joy to come
At length, stumbling home!

Superstition

In fury through the field
The gulls hunt low,
And the clods turn surly
Under the plough.

All night the wind moaned
Under the rooftree,
And owlish voices
Cursed mine and me;

Earth's creatures united
Through night and morn
Lamenting the moment
That I was born.

Who am I to defy them;
What strength is mine,
With the gods many and fickle,
And their will divine?

The Death of the Irises

What day was that in June
When the wind with a southern tune
Rattled the hard small cherries,
Shook the close gooseberries,
And bellied full the fans of lime
Toward the odorous evening time?
It was the day whose noon was skied
With sheets of lead, bolted and tied
By seams of levin.   Hailstones scarred
The tender green, and battered hard
Upon the irises, poor maids,
Who fell, and died on their own blades.

But all that metal mischief done,
Peace returned with the setting sun.
The stately clouds with silver crest
In vast perspective to the west
Sailed off, and left the vaulted blue
Serene, eternal, with its bright
Rainwashed delirium of light.
The muted blades conspired to hide
Fear-engendered suicide.

Winter Gratitude

To the revelation of November-naked nests
In elm-top and hawthorn,
I return from my summer friendship with the birds.
Shy and unwitting, they uplifted my sorrow
With irrelevant song from their inhuman breasts,
Music by thought untorn,
Untroubled by the memory of words,
Voicing no yesterday and no to-morrow.

Now they are gone, even the robin subdued;
Even the trooping finches flitting in the hedgerows
Plane forlornly to earth and are lost in the furrows.

And yet I revisit their haunts as a man renewed,
Striding through hollow woodlands with mind spilling over
Its seed of joy, as a sower swings over the fallows
Scattering the future corn and the honey-filled clover.

153

Caprice in Trafalgar Square

Yesterday the sun came flirting to the fountains;
Lifting their tresses through a golden comb,
Laughing and kissing those white-haired virgins,
Bold as a god can be, knowing no shame.

To-day he is vanished, clouded and thoughtful;
And the naiads are forgotten.   O Genius of Light,
While you linger aloof, brooding new creation,
Pity these virtuous pillars of salt!

A Dream at Middle Age

At noonday, unexpected in the noise,
    I fell upon a mood of morning-thought,
And saw two whispering and ardent boys
    Planning some rare design, with timber brought
From an old barn tumbled beneath the elms.
    They were to build a galleon for each,
And set their sails, and lean upon their helms
    Across the wide Equator, to the beach
Of some surf-thundering haven in the South
    Where koko-palms leaned over the lagoon.
There would they land, and seek with parching mouth
    A rock-pool snowed with the dissolving moon.
When did that wild adventure go aground;
Where is that spring no mortal ever found?

The Cornish Cliff

Night fell on the open sea;
And the ancient harbour folded
Its arms.   One, two, and three,
The lamps in cottage windows gleamed
Down the dark water, shook, and streamed,
While the last gull scolded.

It was not safe to linger then
On that crag above the foam.
There were cries of drowning men,
Deep Atlantic furies shrieking
In long-vanished shrouds, death-seeking!
Through the windless air we battled home.

Myth

The dark-skinned boy lay on a level mound
Where mighty Ganges met the mightier sea.
The halting ships, outward and homeward bound,
Dipped to his turbaned music.   Could it be
The mermaids' song, the half-crazed mariners cried,
Their tarry ropes neglected in their hands;
Could this sad, human melody be blown
From conches out of lips by sea-foam dyed?

Their query trembled to the sun-bleached sands
And perished there.   The ships passed down unknown,
Bearing the myth to a stranger, northern world,
Of unlocated trafficking between
The porpoise and his dancing cousin, curled
And scented with sea-lavender, and green
With broidery of pale and sodden weed,
A sea-king's daughter by no mortal seen
Except the destined victims of her greed.

The Enemy of Man

Fangs gleaming in the sun,
    The ocean-tiger lay,
Between the horizon
    And the bay.

Deep in his silver mane
    I lingered with fearless limb,
But the terror half-insane
    With which Man watches him,
Lurked in my brain.

A Receipt

Let us be easy in our verse,
    As Horace was, or Martial:
But not give outward praise or curse,
    Though personally partial
To this or that idea, or face,
    With secret bias for a friend,
A politic, or hidden place.
    No matter!   Let the poem end
Serenely, and with grace.

An Exile

I saw the queen of that lost country pass.
Though she was far beyond her loyal bounds,
I knew her by her grace.   She trod the grass
As though she held in leash her restive hounds—
And yet before her nothing but the dew.
Her princely hands were idle by her side.
Late treachery and ruin I could view
Carven in pallor on her cheek and brow.
This, and the chill of morning made her pride
Shine only purer, without the pompous taint
Of royalty crowned.   She went so humbly now;
A fallen queen exalted to a saint.

Plague

No longer let me mirror
The world of sea and air,
For moon and stars have vanished,
And nothing ventures there.

The tides are down and tethered,
The shores with salt are dry;
The sun goes gloomed and sulphured
Across the faded sky.

What plague of ancient evil
Has now beset the Earth,
That has nor rain or sunshine,
And Man no tears or mirth?

The Little Faith

Too soon we gave our hearts to grief,
    And looked on death to find
But sorrow for a life so brief
    And beauty left behind.

We lost the world but lately found,
    Too eager in our greed,
Unsculpturing the petals bound
    About the deathless seed.

Sufficient, at the end, to learn
    Through man's divine despair
That as our hope's last treasures burn
    The phoenix trembles there.

A Dream of Royalty

Suppose, upon the midnight of my mind
After the disillusionment of day,
I should by chance encounter on the way
A queen with garments streaming in the wind,
A queen but lately widowed of her land
And throne, now crying out for me to stay,
Succour her princeling, moaning with lips grey,
'Do this, and you shall kiss our royal hand.'

Should I, the proud republican, decline
That favour, forging a doctrine out of this
To spurn the mother for her tumbled crown?
Or would my deeper dreaming self divine
The greater royalty of grief, and down
On humble knee, touch the salt hand, and kiss?

The Last Gift

It was enough, to see her walk away
Out of the room, out of his world of life.
He bowed, submissive to the deathly stroke;
But courtesy was cruel at the edge,
A knife secreted in a rebel's hand.
Farewell! Farewell! rang wildly in his heart.
But hatred was the echo that returned!
And then he knew her absence utterly,
Knew that all sympathy and gentleness
Were gone with her, leaving him hard of heart,
A prince without a kingdom of content,
With none to serve him, and with none to serve.

'O Mother of Desire and Queen of Thought'
He cried, while grief snatched back the words to silence,
'Not to be named, elusive to the end
Of time, of life, and individual hope:
To king his people, to poet his despair,
Law to the statesman, Woman to all men;
Now I have lost you, and in losing, found!

Bereaved, who dreamed of marriage and delight;
Rewarded thus, with nothing for my faith,
I take your final gift of love's negation,
And now am rich with emptiness.   Farewell.'
Thereat he sheathed the rebel knife again,
And turned to sanctitude, and peace of heart.

The Musician at Rest
(*In memory of John Edward Church*)

They have come with the musician;
They have put him out of sound,
Into his silent sleeping place
Under the ground.

The snow in its quiet rhythm
Has hung with soundless tune
A symphony round about him
Of quilt and dune.

How lovely the echo of music
That lingers about his grave,
Echo of the singing thoughts
He shaped, and gave.

Large and free as the passion
That shone from his hand and brain
Is the passage of frost and flowers,
Of sun and rain.

He had such store of riches,
They have spilled and overflown
The baskets of the gleaners
Who come down alone,

Who come after the harvest,
His full melody of life,
To gather the cadences of peace
Fallen from strife.

Entreaty Unanswered

How far have you wandered
In three years of death,
Beyond the grave's gateway
And last road-sign of breath?

It seems, by comparing,
That those whom you left,
Have stood still, bewildered,
Frozen, bereft!

You may not regret this;
Maybe you forget
The Earth stiff and static
Where the eagles fret:

Blood, that sleep-potion;
And the indolent brain,
The leaden equipment
Of us who remain.

Such paraphernalia
And gross weight you dropped
At our hearts-side that moment
When your breathing stopped.

O Ganymede, vanished,
In MIND to carouse,
Have you no message
For our clod-rooted house?

In After-years

She sits beside our hearth,
The girl I wooed so long
With ardour and despair.
Time has touched her gently,
Put silver in her hair,
And left her lips their mirth.
The ghost of childhood's song
Still lingers on her breath.
Yet we have bowed together
Before the harshest weather
That blows from life to death
And storms across the hill
Where lies our chosen path.
O Time, continue gently
With her beside our hearth,
For I must woo her still!

I watched you vanish down the escalator,
Gliding transfixed, an elegy of motion.
Who, in that mad, electric universe
Could think two lovers parted thus, their hearts
Aching with faith and the deep burden of joy?
But such were you and I, by circumstance
Doomed for some days to go our separate paths,
Each in our lonely ways to dream of the other,
React the word, the glance, the touch of hands,
The secret intimations of understanding
Which make the world again grow young and simple,
A trysting-place between the day and night
With hemispheres of dew, bird-joy, blossom,
And songs of morning when proud kings and poets
Went indistinguishable in their crowns
To take their white princesses to their hearts
And thus set forth to achieve kingdoms, and song!

Ah!   As motionless you vanished into hell,
Into the bright electric hell of underground
Where stood the slot-machines for sentinels
With lips of brass, and all their harsh viscera
Exposed behind their belly-walls of glass,
Lamplit and shameless, gurgitating coins;
I cried within my soul against the theft,
Half mad, half comic, of your love-created,
Love-generating beauty, warm and pulsing,
Changing from beat to beat of the heart within,
As clouds change, or wild flowers in the wind,
Or the breast feathers of the startled bird,
Or anything that nature has endowed
With her mysterious breath, and touched with hands
Invisible, but firm as were Pygmalion's
When out of stone he shaped the flesh and blood,
The mantling thought and shyness of Galatea!

Had I not cause enough to be afraid,
Watching you vanish slowly down the angle,
Fast bound by cords no human eye could see,
Your wistful face upturned, bidding farewell
In wordless agony to the light of day,
To Mother Earth's sane surface, and to one
Who lately held you through the primitive night
In mood of love, falling to effortless sleep,

Dreaming of leaves and waters unmolested
By these new forces of unrusting steel,
These demons of electric machination
Depriving us of hand, of foot, of brain,
Forcing us back to state of chrysalis,
Binding us mummified away from the sun,
Half-living shuttles hurling to and fro
Within the loom of underground?
                                    Farewell,
Modern Eurydice!   Watching you vanish,
My heart stopped as the cold illusion grew
That we were parting at this monster's bidding,
You to return for ever to its keeping;
Your wayward beauty, of warm flesh and blood,
And all your lavish gifts of irrational love
Denied and fastened by electric law.
What wonder that your face shone to the sky
Pale, wistful, as though vanishing for ever!

Brunette

I would not take a princess all men know,
To lose the secret gipsy of my heart.
The rusted scarf, the eyes as wild as death,
Her hands, those small companions of the sun,
Her breasts, hanging like grapes of Italy,
Her glancing limbs, more adept in love's art
Than all the courtesans of ancient Greece
With whom the great philosophers grew wise
In dalliance, while the classic mornings dawned
And made their joys immortal as their thoughts.

For what I have of her, no man has seen!
She is a vixen to the world, her eyes dishonest,
Her hands too sharp and treacherous to trust,
Her breasts unknown, but venomous and bitter,
Her limbs elusive and as strong as snakes.
No throne upon a kingdom grown polite
Would hold the secret gipsy of my heart!

The Complaint

I can do no more!
I gave all I possessed;
My poverty, my treasure
Of pride, thought, leisure,
Ambition, all the rest
Of riches man strives for
To pacify his terror!

But these were not enough;
My ghosts, my wealth of air,
My worship and my faith.
You could not use a wraith
For your adornment, wear
Such unsubstantial stuff
To gratify your mirror!

The Oath

It is not now the mode
To swear by beauty's eyes,
But I would swear by yours,
With their deep amours,
Their truth most treacherous,
Their revealing lies.

Enough that I have owed
So much, and given more,
Languished and laboured there,
Let passion leap, and dare
Presume on genius,
Learning love's lore.

The Difference

If we were gods at play,
We should exclaim at this
Pause between kiss and kiss,
'Sport has been good to-day!'
And laughing, pass on our Olympian way.

But being human, bound
By the capricious pull
Of laws all-powerful
Blood-fettered to the ground,
We feel, 'twixt kiss and kiss, death's dripping wound.

The Dead Poet

Before the caverns of the Sun
I woke when mortal life was done,
A creature so compact of fire
That I was master of desire;
In my unterrestrial frame
Consuming the prison-cords of shame,
Annihilating dross of Earth
Within this Heracleitan birth:
Proud from the flaming womb of light,
A Phoenix, lifting in my flight
High over Earth subdued and paled,
The self who there had tried and failed.

Then and Now

I hear the gate catch and latch, but now
It is an echo thirty years ago.
Here where I sleep in life, the droning planes,
The traffic of minted gold, the fevered gains
In time and pace, I join a later race,
Men not as men were then, but slower and dark;
Yes, moving it seems—but this may be my dream's
Illusion; through sleep the scene is murk,
The sun slowed, the moon tarnished, the stars
But muted candles mirrored in the streams
Sliding between the mountains and the firs.

All that I see and hear is mirror-scenes,
Mirror-sounds; no straight glance, no sun-shaft
Falling direct upon a blazing flower;
Nothing so bright or candid; eyes averted,
And even a laugh—if any could have laughed—
Withdrawn and shoulder-hidden, a shade lower
Than present life.   Thirty years have parted
That mirth from this my hearing.   There is left
A meagre percolation through opaque
Time.   I do not wonder these things make
But faint seeming of what they were, or are,
Since having crept from then to now, they break
The laws of Time, the invisible tyrant, shake
His dynasty founded on forgetfulness.

To remember, to see as I see now, the star
Diminished in the pool, the moon tarnished,
The sun dimmed, even so is a conquest,
Capturing vanished kings and their dead pride,
And taking to my present humble breast
The poisoned Cleopatra for a bride,
And setting the crowns again upon the towers
Of Ilium; yes, and garnishing a feast
Of Eden fruits in the morning of mankind:
And of my own frail thirty years not least,
Gathering with dew on them the book-pressed flowers
Whose odour faded long before the love
That now is faded, too.
                              Such are the powers
Of memory, king of kings, Death's treasurer.
And yet some say man is no measurer
Of eternity, which lacking time and space,
Never converges into now, yet passes hence
Into life vanished, where the moon is tarnished,
The sun dimmed, the stars veiled in grace,
Where opposites have found a trysting-place,
Sorrow with joy, light with dark, age with youth,
To share at last the ripened fruit of truth
And overturn false destiny and fate.

This is our triumph, we who dwell with pain,
That by the dream-borne latching of a gate
We spin the dying universe again.

Dangerous Friendships

I too, knew Socrates for friend,
And paced beneath the lance-leaved grove,
Greeting with him the famous men
Who passed with their boy-lovers, deep
In converse amorous and wise.
We gave the road to chariots,
To athletes haughty in their pride,
And stopped for Alcibiades
To mouth his latest boast, and leer
At the lewd women caught in war.

But many greetings could not break
The web of the Socratic mind,
The perfect fabric I might touch
As though I were an Indian girl
Stroking with finger-tips the silk
That make great Alexander pause
To feast his eyes on indolent beauty
Defying him and all his conquests.

O useless moments lost in wisdom,
The idleness that made us gods;
Leaving mere living, daily bread,
Ambition and the need of place,
Desire for family and rank,
Awhile unto more virtuous men
Whose prudence should restrain their thoughts
From intellectual wanderings,
From passions of the mind, from love
Between the disembodied souls
Of fools too careless to consider
The hunger of the day, the joy
At midnight in a woman's arms,
And seats of honour in the Senate.

The Hand-glass of Death

If time were telescoped, the adventure of love
Might picture as the preening of a wing,
A bee's debate before the flower's womb.
For love is not so rich in its events.
It has to count on a few, lonely deeds;
The first encounter; the debate of mind
Over the quick rebellion of the blood;
The failure of that council, the recourse
To darker advocates; the second failure.
Then follow the acquaintance and confession,
The little gestures of the virgin bodies;
Touch of hand, averted glance, and flush
Of shame guilty of its own innocence.

But these are dews that vanish in the heat
When passion suddenly flings its morning beams.
Thereafter all its boldness, generous giving,
And hunger that feeds upon itself, like fire
Falling inward to engulfing flame.
Then from the ash the little phoenix rises,
A timid charity with fluttered wings,
A bird of quiet companionship, who lingers
About the house and garden of quiet marriage,
Until in course of time its feathers fall,
And its eyes, so long bead-bright with sympathy,
Cloud over, tremble, and at last are locked.

Thereafter the blind house remains awhile
Unspirited, except for breath of wings
Beating in the memory, making commotion
That is the negative of things remembered;
Joy in recollection being pain,
Sorrow a gratitude, mistrust a faith,
And the last loss a most revealing union.
For death begins with cheat!   Having come, and taken,
He leaves a numbness in the mind, suggesting
All is vanished that was ever quick
Between two souls who knew the harmony
Half heard in the communion of the flesh.

But that is death's deception!   Soon revives
All that now lies beyond the grave; deeds, thoughts,
Conquest and gift, and little usuries
Such as love dabbles in for its enrichment,
And love's own griefs so often self-created:
All these re-pass before the lethean mirror
Left in the hand of memory, death's gift
That proves of greater worth than sorrow first
Dared hope, being magician over time,
And conjuror with space, framing the universe
Wherein love's recent story was enacted.
And thereby giving it accentuation,
Making the human action show divine,
With man and woman the twin halves of God.

Horace in Old Age

Tonsured by time, not faith,
Old Horace yet can raise
A querulous note of praise
Through gaps of vanished teeth.

Neaera's eyes grow dim
With passion as she listens,
And all her wild hair glistens
With dangers not for him.

Dreaming of one not there,
She leans her head, and learns
How love at music burns,
Though age contrives the air.

Silence

Ah!   Quiet in the woodland!
The beech trees are still.
The cloud-shadows wander
Over the hill.

No sound from the robin
In the hawthorn alone,
Last singer of autumn,
The swallows gone.

Even the river,
Shallow with mirth
And song of the pebbles,
Has sunk to earth.

Farewell to the reaper;
Farewell to the sun.
The tumult is over,
The task is done.

Tell us a tale of the eternal heart,
Miraculous fountain of legend.
We are ready to forget that boughs bend
No longer under lading of fruit,
But whip and whine before the dart
Flowing from the icy-fingered east,
Heralding want and hunger.   Human kind,
Since first emerging from the wave-born yeast
Into the poisoned paradise of Mind
Has learned of fraud that comes before the fruit,
The serpent in the glade, the canker
In the core, the stumble in pursuit,
The sudden lethargy in strength.

But still in day-dream our thoughts hanker
After the golden apple to be won
Through days of fabulous length
Whose light is gathered from no actual sun
But streams from godhead where Apollo burns
Upon his throne of merit,
Soul of Earth's soul, the solar spirit.

There, in that wheel behind the cycle of sense,
Is type of all things here,
The harness of our labour through the year,
The plough, the basket, and the subtle wrist,
The harrow and the horn,
The lip-dewed vapour of the harvest-morn,
The reaper with the scythe, the twist
Gathering the golden shock,
The vat, the granary, the flock
And udder-laden herd,
The gleaner and the unforbidden bird.

These are of that world behind the world
Where no corruption creeps;
Where sorrow, even as it weeps
Is glorious with courage; where desire
Is by swift alchemy compounded
From fettered lust into creative fire,
And where our broken hopes are rounded
Into the architecture of the Word,
The pantheon of legend where are seated
The god by our own mouths and thoughts created,
And our eternal tale of hope is heard.

PART SEVEN

TWELVE NOON

1936

The Wych-elm

In weariness of heart,
Bitter with false labour,
I put the world apart
And seek an old neighbour.

A century or more
He has mused and murmured
Over my door
Of what the winds rumoured.

I am never tired
Of his leaf-lippings,
Garrulous, absurd
In his bough-whippings.

He will rub his branches
Like a musing fly,
Though his great haunches
Are three cottages high.

He will squeak in the night
Like a foraging mouse,
And tremble with fright
Above the house.

He will affront the moon
With antics of folly,
And next day at noon
Sham green melancholy.

As I say to the woman
Who shares my cottage,
'The tree's almost human
In its whimsical dotage!'

Strange to be home from the woods.
The streets are brittle and hard
To nerves grown gentle to moss
And the tread of leaf-mould.
Here are faces and words,
Wheels and the glitter of print:
Deep, irreconcilable loss
Of the soft swing of beech boughs,
The under-gleam, the glint
Of green fire, the subtle fold
Of bud-scales and wings of birds,
The roof-music as the wind soughs
In larch spires and canopy of green.

Is it true that yesterday we trod
Those silent floors, and were seen
Talking with the velvet god
Of moles and mice, our sight
Touched with panic immortality
In a world leaf-hidden from the sky,
Bewizarded with century-shaded light?

The Bonfire

God of gardeners, accept this coil
Of acrid smoke from nettle and weed,
This left-hand mound of sinful soil
That I have sifted from the seed.

With hoe and mattock, spade and rake,
From morning dew to evening grace,
My back has bended for Thy sake,
To bring sweet order to this place.

Thy fruits and tubers basketed,
Thy flowers lit from setting sun,
With fragrant heart and reverent head
I tend this altar gleaming red,
As my forefathers must have done.

The Unrealists

I do not wish again
To venture in the air.
I am old, and every bone
In its socket must groan,
As I pass from the pain
Of the bed to the chair.

And yet I recall
How I covered the land,
How I mastered the sea,
Such strength to my knee
And power to my hand,
That I dreaded no fall.

Who are these twain,
The young and the old;
What person are they
Who meeting to-day
Each other enfold,
And vanish again?

The Silent Tower

Not a word uttered; not a word!
Only the straining rope is heard
Pulled in the tower of thought,
Shaking the bells of the mind.
But I lack strength, I who have sought
To cast word-music on the wind,
Summon the expectant crowd
With certainty, with loud
Joy and clangour of song
Triumphant, faith-bringing, and strong.

Vain hope; feeble hands gripping
Ropes of words that round not
Over the bells that sound not.
I hear only my thoughts slipping
Like mice in the silent tower
That should be throbbing with power
Of deep-tongued music hurled
Out and fulfilling the world
Which has waited over-long
For the challenge and leadership of song.

Summer

Once more the miracle of leaves
Brings youth into the blood,
Persuading the experienced man
That 'beautiful' and 'good'
Are more than words half understood.

Within his tower of self he hears
His five senses ring
Revolt against the laws of Time,
And he puts on an angel's wing
And foots it in the slime.

Midsummer Night

No sound!   No sound!
    The city sleeps.
Fear like a footpad
    Nearer creeps.
Velvet-coated,
    Soft of tread,
Dreams come slipping
    Over my head.

Now it is midnight!
    The heavy throat
Of the song-bird sorrows
    Note over note.
While the ancient, heavy
    Scent of the bine
Burdens my spirit
    With grief not mine.

Dawn

Strange to leave the secret joy
And light a candle in the dark,
To grope toward the door, and stay
In fear before a world frost-grey,
While thoughts of sullen duty lurk
Behind the tremor and touch of sleep,
And memory of a whispered gift.
Was it this made Psyche weep,
And Eros linger as he left?

Sleep's Familiar

Sleep, you say, is benign; but beneath
Dreams rout, and the arch-dream death.
Those you dare not speak about, you turn
Your eyes, and ears, and hungry mouth away,
Refusing to believe, refusing to learn.

Command your fears, let the truth burn
Down to the bone.　Then from the grey
Ash of fear, and the cold ash of flesh,
Conjure your skeleton to rise, and find
The sleepless road, the deathless road.
Love that is fearless will not mind.

The Apple Tree

A tree big with apples
Is a comfortable sight,
Standing like a woman
In the autumn light,
Her burden so heavy
Beneath her green leaves,
That for shame she hides it
Under drooping branches,
Under folded sleeves.

Nocturne

This shall be for a hymn
When the house is asleep.
Silence shall hear it; the dim
Lamp, the dull fire, the deep
Owl-sentried darkness beyond
The panes, the orchard, the pond;
These shall hear it, further it
With hissing of wick,
Falling of charcoal stick,
With mousing beak;
And then, since it is human and weak,
Benight it, smother it!

Birthplace

Are you from the island too?
Were you born in the nether cave,
Laid on samphire, washed with dew,
And salt spray from the breaking wave?

No! The secret of my birth
Is not hidden over-sea;
I am child of forest-earth,
And the mountain suckled me.

Peace in the Underground

Standing quietly on the escalator
In the dear silence of the din,
How good it was to scan the posters,
And feel no prick beneath the skin.

To be alone in the wheels' thunder,
The tread of feet, the thread of voices;
A garden-god, a philosopher
In a solitude of ten paces.

Delay

The grass is clotted still
Upon the hill.
No springtime metal
Of yellow petal
Has yet been scattered.
Snow-spattered
Is the only motley.
O Sun, shine hotly!

The Immortal

With dying fire and light,
With agony of birds
The day defers to the night,
And thought descends to words.

Immortal might become
The poet who could take
The rapture that is dumb,
And simple music make.

Joys of Disillusionment

Youth has no men, no lovers true,
But only heroes, only gods.
Its forest leaves but imitate
The trembling of lost poets' words.
Its revelations are not new.
The moments when it waxes great
Are others it would emulate.

O welcome the experience
That slays the god and sears the dream,
That changes the enchanted grove
To common woodlands, and reduces
Heroes to men of sober sense,
Who find that passion has its uses
When pendulous with work and love.

The End

Soon, when the Sun despairs in heaven,
And space and time go blind,
War and wisdom, love and folly
Shall drop from humankind.

No heat to rouse their dead desire,
No light to lead their pride;
The sons of men shall vanish then,
The guided with the Guide.

Choosing the Epitaph

Grave on this limestone slab the praise of death;
Conjure a rhyme ignoring him who lies
In sleep so deep that even his lustful eyes
Have lost their fire, as lips have lost their breath.
Broken the balance of three elements,
Fire, air, and water welded into one;
For now into the last they all have run.
His bones are water, and each passionate sense
Has long dissolved therein and flowed to earth
Stained with the chemistry of mortal life,
The sullied mirth, the grief, the ease and strife,
Quietly accumulated since his birth.
So neither praise nor pity him who lies
Filtered through death to separate purities.

The Tree Gazer

Lying level beneath the elm,
Up-looking through the leaves,
I consume some twenty years,
And haunt other groves.
Through eighty seasons, green and sere,
Budding and falling, I return,
Finding a sweeter wisdom there,
Faiths that more unwavering burn
Than belief and knowledge here.

I would ask what subtle potion
Time from twenty years distils,
That an inexperienced youth
Should be wiser and more trustful
Than this present, prone, unrestful
Dreamer drunk on an odd notion.
I look up into green wells,
Half discerning the untruth.

Second Birth

Sweet counsel this, to die, and be born again,
To grope among the sleeping graves awhile
With charnel thoughts and murmurings of pain,
And then return to walk upon the earth
Still blind, and shaking out the odour of death.

For the first birth is lost in sleep and hunger.
Flesh is too new and too adventurous;
It will not wait to savour what it knows,
For it knows nothing, recognizes none,
Cries only to devour, makes blood of milk.

But at this second coming we come with peace:
We are content to stand apart and watch,
Waging no conflict, glad without desire,
Blessed with the miracle of water into wine,
And cunning as an ancient faun with rumours
Of immortal changes, and a smothered traffic
Unceasing between nothingness and men.

An Autumn Night

To-night some strange excitement in the stars
Troubled the heavens: seams of broken light
Trembled, parted, and through the livid scars
Shades of sidereal glory, ghostly bright,
Beat pinions, and archangels might be seen
By every groundling creeping home to bed.
No slipper-minded soul, however mean,
But stayed his step, and lifted up his head
To marvel at the wonder, and behold
For once with Milton's eyes the hierarchies
From Godhead, rank by rank, wheel and unfold
Their old mysterious order to his eyes.
Alas!   Though visible to all mankind,
No blind and singing Milton could they find!

The Last Evening

This is the last evening we shall spend amongst the flowers,
The oxlips, the cowslips, the laughing yellow flowers
Loving in the woods, in their brown bed of leaves,
Silent in their pleasure, bedded on the leaves.

This is the last evening we shall hear the blackbird shout
Songs of the world's boyhood, songs he used to shout
To Adam in the Garden when the world was young.
For now we go to London, and London is not young.

Grace before Meat

Before I lived I took this knife in hand,
Consumed this unborn flesh upon the plate:
Went further, saw the glitter of the sand
Cohering into clay, following fate
Toward the potter's wheel.   Now what I eat
Is but a barmecide, yet for the day
Sufficient, a material deceit
To carry truth upon its ancient way.
Behold how pitiful the parted lips
That crave to satisfy a hunger grown
Out of the passion set 'twixt Adam's hips
Long ere the individual was known.
O Giver of this food, make it Thy blood,
To feed the mind that has not understood.

Man-Child

There is nothing I fear now
After these years;
For I can hear now
The changing of tears,
Their changing to joy.
I have lost the old sorrow,
The grief of a boy.

Oh, foolish to tell me
That childhood is bright;
I recall what befell me,
More shadow than light;
And shadow so black,
Even now I must tremble,
And dare not look back.

Lunar Eclipse

The Moon is gone!
I see the swollen shade
Of my thick body
Swallow up the Sun;
My body dead, and laid
Upon the Earth, its bier;
While pacing, pacing,
Borne with taper-stars,
The Bearers of the World,
Their arms interlacing,
Their triumph furled,
Pass—and the Moon shines clear!

The Huntress

Good-bye!   Good-bye!   I see the hooves
Spark upon the stone,
And the great lady with hooded hair
Has wheeled her horse and gone.

She has gone hunting with the hounds
To beat the world for prey.
She who was gentle love last night,
Has whipped, spurred, and away!

A fool, a madman found this tree
Whereunder you stand.
He recognized a woodland bee
That rested on his hand.

He breathed upon its golden sacks
To ease it of its load,
And followed down leaf-rotten tracks
Along the forest road.

It led him like a patient beast
Where no man ever trod,
And bade him welcome to the feast
With bear, and bird, and god.

In that quaint company he fed,
And slumbered there, replete,
To wake with wings, a poet's head,
And clawed and hairy feet.

Aspirin

Jangled nerves, snuggle down
Like lover with lover;
The knife is withdrawn,
The threat has passed over.
Rest, rest!   Sink into sleep;
There was a gathering of sheep
In a meadow by a stream,
And the gentle cattle moved
Slowly wading through the reeds
Where the broody moorhen lived,
And the willow blossom shook
A drug of golden seeds
On the scholar's open book,
While the learned man slept on
Easy as a child at breast,
All his hard-won knowledge gone,
All his ignorance at rest.

Reading

I read beneath the trees
Green philosophies,
Thought-shadows
Lay in the meadows,
Songs on the river.

I turned the page over,
And the sun went out.
Clouds gathered with doubt,
The river ran blind
Through the grey land,
I read beneath the trees
Dead philosophies.

The Gardener in Autumn

Creating smoke-powder to no man's order,
Nor serving altar, nor filling larder,
I feed the leaves to the unsacred flame;
Restless with freedom, content with shame,
Over the lifted fork dreaming of duty
And my old service.

But now in the fire
I watched the phoenix-struggle of past beauty,
The writhing, the change over the dropped desire;
The shrivelling weeds, the petals from the plucked flowers,
All fruits of long labour, of deep faith, now coiling
Upward in a column of lavender this autumn morning.
And I, the gardener, death in my heart, watch them burning;
These that I fought, these that I reared with such toiling
In a vanished life, in forgotten hours.

This is no new way to expiate the crime
Of growing old, of being passed in the race
Run by the generations, father and son.
I plead no guilt, regret no squandered time,
Admit of no defeat.
Merely I stand alone in this private place,
Watching the revelation of light and heat,
Awaiting the mound of ash now the work is done

The Promise

At Michaelmas the purple daisy-dust
Shakes in the mist and falls heavy with rain.
We have had enough of apples and grain,
Great ricks and threshing, hedge-cider and crust.
Our muscles ache; we have survived the lust
Of the sun, stirring in artery and vein
Madness and longing.   Autumn has come again,
And the old earth turns over, smelling of must.

Into gloom she rolls, but we being more
Than her creatures, look to another fire,
Another summoning of blood.   Desire
Still burns within us, mounting to the mind.
That is light which was but heat before,
And we hear music in the leaf-strown wind.

Traveller's Comment

I thought that when the wine of youth was done,
The dreams and joyful terrors would subside,
Leaving me to a jog-trot noonday ride
Across a ripening plain warmed by the sun,
While greeting passing neighbours one by one,
Nor downcast if by mischance none replied,
Nor proud if one with admiration cried
And stopped to flatter me, ere passing on.

But middle-age proves not so smooth a path.
I still behold, at dusk of common day,
Light beyond light, more heady than youth's wine,
To kindle hopes dark with the final wrath;
While to men's comment on my work and play
My foolish heart hangs judgments half divine.

Alone

There is no solitude but this:
The moon-flooded garden,
And deception of flowers;
The bat-wings' whip and hiss,
Apples aching on the branches;
The cold poplar tree:
All that thought and night blanches;
And the years drowning me.

Drought

The bee in the bugle-flower,
The toad in the trough,
Both search with the dowser
For water enough,
For water, for water
In dusty despair
To loosen the honey,
The ruby, the money.
They search everywhere,
But they fail, and they fall
Waterless, wan;
The honey-dried bee,
The ruby-dull toad,
The money-dragged man,
Each his own road,
But thirsty all three.

Twelve Noon

Time now to run alongside the hours,
Breast to breast with the moments,
Breaking earlier measures.
Morning with moods and inward glances
Has vanished, the beads of the dew
No longer may offer their crystal for gazing
At self in the flowers.
No longer that flush, that shame, those pleasures
And the innocent sin that light of morning enhances,
Converting the stale to the new
And the naïve to self-praising.

With youth all time lay before:
There shone my hope, my confident strength,
While my brain was deceived with the old,
The metres and rhymes of the past.
I revelled with the dead, and debated
With ghosts, nor suspected my problems were cold,
Nor dreaded my fire would not last.
But it is done.   My youth at full length
Lies dead with the dead whom it bore
So gallantly up from the grave.

I shall haunt them no more,
The figures, the dreams, the reputes whom I loved
And served with such passion, not knowing I moved
Within the mast of the prisoning years,
Husks of unscented, unseeded
Pods of the fruit long devoured.

What wonder youth labours unheeded,
So stifled by time that is dead,
So self-overpowered,
Ill-nourished on meats that are shrivelled and bled.
Is it not strange that in the morn of life,
The heart and mind, lacking experience,
Yet both so ardent in the joys of sense,
Both interlocked with clumsy, brotherly strife,
Should fret their nimbleness with chains long rusted
And bind their eyes with handkerchiefs of death
And let unthinking reverence quell their breath
And bid their own brave innocence be distrusted?

But life has many a stranger paradox
Than this of youth trailing clouds of time,
Guarding them like sheep, convention's flocks;
Changing to glory many an ancient crime.
Lips are reluctant to forsake the breast.
The fledgeling falters on the edge of the nest.

But now the ominous strokes of midday boom,
And as the prophetic sound-waves ripple
Over the world, lips leave the nipple,
Wings flutter, and launch into their doom;
And Niobe lifts her eternal cry of sorrow
For children dead to her, slain by to-morrow.

I may look back and pity the mother of mothers.
But I am not of her.   She would retain
Within the womb that darkens, the breast that smothers,
This rich fruit of her lust, this body and brain,
This maker and breaker craving for space,
Prepared to shatter time in the race
Now that the warning has rung.

The lullaby is over, the nursing song is sung,
I swing no more in the cradle of the past.
The branches of the tree no longer shelter me.

I may look back with love, I may cry out
With agony, biting on remorse,
I may accuse myself, and my crime grow worse
As time turns it about
Revealing new facets of despair.
I may be broken by those beseeching hands,
The light so cruel on that fading hair;
But I dare not return to succour her.
For she is implacable, she is allied to the past,
She is the muse of history, a maker of laws
I have grown strong to break
For my own freedom now, and at the last
For her and her descendants' sake,
Refusing her love for love's larger cause.

Here is a monument in ancient form,
O mother of my blood, who at midday
Cries after me because I will not stay,
And by my silence in the twelve strokes' storm,
Deny you, Mother!   Still your breast is warm
Where I have nestled; still I hear you say,
'Peace!   Peace, my child, sleep time away.
Venture not in space.   You shall take no harm.

Mother, whom I repudiate with this
Sonnet for symbol, I must let you grieve,
Give you the son of sons' last treacherous kiss,
And start upon my odyssey of power.
O cry not so upon me as I leave.
Not mine the cruelty.   Blame the noontide hour.

After that second birth, that second weaning,
Solitude blows upon my limbs;
The lonely sun is ruling from his throne
And at his feet the pale sky dims.
I stand upon the earth, alone,
Afraid of my own courage, leaning
No more upon my ruinous thoughts.
The tumbled tower of reason lies behind me,
And old authorities no longer find me
Obedient and docile to their will.
They too are dead.   My birthplace is death.
I have slain myself with knives of shame.
Remorse and disaster have filled me with new breath.

Now I must conquer Troy with body lame
From throes of birth.   For I mean to conquer Troy!
I who was once the true Shakespearian boy
Creeping unwillingly to school!
See how it raises its head, the past!
O fool, fool, let it not recur;
Have you not cried enough to her,
'Woman, what have I to do with thee?'
She praying that the madness would not last?
Even as I resolve to look no more,
The twelfth stroke falls.
The imprisoning city is down, the broken walls
Crumble to my tread.
With light-dazzled eyes I see before
The open lands of the living dead
Who sleep, that I may touch them into life.
They who were a legend shall leap into strife,
And I must share the conflict of my noon,
Even though all the wise words have been said,
Even though the world is a waning moon
Shrinking slowly into lava grey and cold,
Though outer space is but a serpent's skin
And time belies itself in growing old.
Even so I must attack; and I must win.

The Mirror

Madam, the time has come to break the mirror,
Divorce yourself from your reflection.
For truth is incomplete, the likeness lies,
And what was pride will suddenly bring terror.

Yes, beyond the mercury, destruction
Waits upon the accumulated days
You call your life.   Your life is death,
Your husband is a skeleton, his caress
A knifestroke, his fidelity a myth.
The babe you thought so innocent is tearing
Your breast, he also is death's scout.

O break the spell, you are too beautiful,
Gazing upon yourself.   Quick, turn about,
Look anywhere!   Time is not pitiful!

The Contrast

Once it was easeful to write love-songs,
In youthful days, in confusion of flesh.
But now, love is a more various thing:
Steeped in politics, sharing of pain,
A pitiful memory in tropical days,
A friendship and counting of money together,
A failure, a proof, and a promise of triumph.

This knowledge eludes every effort of mind,
And the tongue finds no phrase that rings true to the ear.
Love being fulfilled must go quiet to the grave.

Cowed by Magnitude

At dusk, beside the Mediterranean Sea,
I saw wide wheeling hemispheres of light
Rise from the east and swing high over me
To fall far westward.   Trembling at the sight,
I summoned resolution to discover
Where lay the dreaded axis of this motion.
Imagination rose and wandered over
The crinkled land and downward-curving ocean,
And stared into the vacancy of space
Seeking the heart that set this pulse of fire
To lave each star in its appointed place
With wave on wave of unified desire.
Poor pygmy peering from a pygmy earth!
Could I have seen, what was my effort worth?

Paternity

Dreaming child, what shadow haunts your mind,
That small, new-burnished mirror?
But if I woke you, son, you could not find
Words to dispel that overwhelming terror.

O God, the agony to see that spasm
Torture those lips, those fallen lashes!
'Twixt sleep and life, 'twixt you and me a chasm;
And all my knowledge crumbled into ashes.

The Spendthrift

Fortune is out!
I had my youth to spend,
And like a fool, no doubt,
I thought it would not end.
But day by golden day,
Year by year,
It has dissolved away,
And death draws near.

The world was mine,
To squander at my will,
I bade the day to shine;
The night I made distil
Her silver for my pleasure.
No folly was too dear.
But now time marks my measure,
And death draws near.

Thinker's Folly

Every day I grew more certain
That the life of thought was done.
Who can keep faith with contemplation,
When the politicians shorten
Every hour we call our own?

I knew no peace, no solitude,
Even in my green retreat;
For the noise of state and nation,
Grown incessant, must intrude,
Occupy my mind with folly,
Break my peace with fruitless worry.

I said 'the world is mad with hurry;
How can science build a web,
How can art find calm to hover?
Individual life is over,
Civilization bends and breaks.'

And I wept beneath the trees,
Forgetting the triumph of Socrates
In his death amongst the Greeks.

Gulls over Kensington

High over Kensington a spearhead flight
Of gulls that pierce a young December moon.
They wing toward no Christian festival;
No Child is born for them in Bethlehem;
Nor are they harbingers of peace or war.
They pass above our dynasties and faiths,
Slow-moving in a rhythm that contrives
The ancient motion of the heart of time,
The blood-pulse of the spheres.

                              Hark how they cry
Above the town, the frost-fall of the night,
The beauty of the desolate year, the sombre
Smoke-pall closing in upon the city.

That mournful cry, that drooping flight of wings
On some December afternoon will pass
Before an infant moon toward the dusk;
But under them the creeping mist will close
Around the pools, the marshes, and the ruins
Where this great Christian city once looked up
And through the eyes of one at least, beheld
Old Earth resume her dreadful solitude.

The Incompatibles

If you relent, I am prepared.
I did not know your strength!
How should the waters flow
Back from the marshes where the sun has glared,
Back from their brackish neighbourhood of sea,
Where the foiled plover shrieks above the samphire,
To be reconciled upon their source?

But this you have dared!
You who are water, I who am fire,
Both to our elemental rhythm true:
We might have marred ourselves, grown reconciled,
You to the little flame, I to the rivulet,
Making a hissing marriage of the wild
With the wild!   Did you forget
This possibility of impossibles,
The fiery getting of the flood with child,

I fathering, you mothering a god
Green-eyed and cavern-hearted,
Yet with a fiery arrow shod,
And hair amingling, ripple-parted
As water flows, yet crisp as light?

But you, unnatural, have turned away,
Set back the river to the hills;
And the fire dies, the fire stills
Its flames!   See how they play,
Incurled like buds about their death.
But spare words, spare breath.
Hark to the elegy of birds in the tree,
While the light shrinks above, and the waters beneath
Close their mirror.
What has this terror for you, for me?

The Fear

I think she must be dead,
That woman I once heard
Singing like a bird
In the morning overhead.

For I know all things die,
This knowledge I have learned
From moments slowly burned
Into my memory.

I cannot hear a song
In joy's dawn and delight,
But I foresee the night
Shadows creeping along.

I dare no longer trust
The promises of heaven,
For all that life has given,
Death gathers into dust.

Contracted to the compass of my hand
I hold a century of years.
Of that treasure,
Forty I can measure,
Pale skeletons of my experience.
The rest are legendary, I stand
Peering at my palm, and what it bears
Is but the chaff of other men's desires,
Husks of their wheat.
Time seems so long.　It is a cheat,
Raging and passing swifter than straw-fires,
Quicker than thought can follow after sense,
Like treachery of water, or like love
That makes the swallows statues as they move.
But love is only treacherous because
Time hurries it with such confusing laws.
Time is to blame, not love;
Time with quicksilver tongue, that mouths
A passing mockery, making old men of youths,
Putting children in the place of lust
And ripening them, and ageing them before
The tottering lovers dare to trust
Such emblems of their passion,
And cudgel still to find some other fashion
More lasting than those children they once bore.
But they cannot.　Their fires are but an ember.
Time has blown too swiftly on that flame.
Before they know, they find they can't remember,
They and their love are gone without a name,
Interred two generations deep,
Without an answer, but content and calm,
Winnowed by eternal sleep,
And now a legend lying in my palm.

At a Bedside

This is more real than death,
Thus to foretell it;
With sicknurse breath
Mouth the grim word, spell it
Upon fear's alphabet
In heart's blood wet.

Nothing is left but to watch
By day and by night
The piteous, ill-balanced match,
The quenching of light;
All that was joyous, free, brave,
Being dragged to the grave.

Reckless

What a fine funeral!
All six-cylinder cars
Smooth as black velvet,
Fit for a millionaire,
Yet it's only a clerk,
A semi-detached
Who has closed his account,
Paid his last premium,
Safe as a house.
This is his first
Wanton extravagance,
Subtle and rich;
His only adventure.

Fireside

Snuff the candle of your wit,
Dull philosopher.
Blow upon your thought
Till it reddens from a blur
Of smoke, glows, is wrought
To incandescence where sits
White-hot ecstasy that shines
With fiery metals from the mines
Of knowledge richer than the span
Of the narrow seam of man.

With this fragile heat and light
Shield your spirit from the night:
For the darkness ever encroaches:
Yes, the unknown shade approaches.
Do you shiver where you sit?

Pity the Blind

Pity the blind man.   Pity the blind
Who cannot see the grey-haired grass,
Or watch the long limbs of the wind
Dancing about the clouds as they pass
Autumn-bosomed and serene.

Pity the blind because he has not seen
The dawn, the day, the night,
And all the little follies of the light
When it assumes an odour, counterfeits
A sound, and calls for fingers, not for sight.

Pity the blind when darkness meets
With shadow, in double oblivion
Shrouding the world, waking a ghost,
While senses shrink and wind is lost,
And the soul hesitates—is gone!

Pity the blind with bright and perfect sight
Who stares upon the empty earth and skies,
Believing in the evidence of eyes,
And has not seen that treachery and flight.

The Spell

I knelt upon a stone
And listened to the song
Of a linnet in a bush.
I had not listened long
Before the music stopped,
And there I knelt alone
Still in the after-hush
Entranced.   And when I woke
I found the summer gone,
The leaves upon the oak
Shrivelled, grey with frost.
Then, one by one, they dropped,
And I was old and lost.

One Man's Life

I read the poems of a man, whom, rumour
Whispered, was dying of a tumour,
Not in himself, but in the woman
Who sought to make his life more human.

She made him bear her pains.
By proxy in his reins
She agonized herself into that man,
And in his veins her poison ran.

She would wake in the night for her sin
And scream aloud, and draw him in
To ease her torment, swearing she would die
With issue, though she knew that was a lie.

Next day he would not write, no visitation
Of glory would flower from his contemplation.
He would be sterile, and she pleased,
Feeling her fear gone, her pain eased.

An evil course for life to take; a river
Dammed; beauty thrown back upon the giver;
Heart-cheering song changed to an anodyne;
Man marred to make a woman's medicine.

The Blind Scholar

These eyelids, growing old,
Need props.   But there are none.
I was mad, when young,
To barter muscle for knowledge,
Even this small tissue of the eye.
For darkness surely is death,
And knowledge is not sure.

O to be a fool treading the field,
Staring half-witted to the numbered sky!
I'd give my mathematics for that moment,
And shed my grammar like a garment,
To gain his eyes once more.

Excuse

Do you understand,
Critic, philosopher,
The patience of the man
Ploughing his land,
His wheat grown and gone,
A season's wealth won?

To be rich is to be poor,
Critic, philosopher.
All things come once;
Love, glory, something more;
But then, for recompense,
Wisdom shall turn dunce.

From full down to fallow,
Critic, philosopher,
Such is the farmer's rote
Which we all must follow:
So blame not the throat
That sang, but sings not.

Early Wisdom

Had we been wise at birth,
We might have learned upon the breast
From the heart beating without rest,
What danger lies in sleep,
What treachery in mirth.

In that blood-pulse, dark and deep,
We should have heard the tread
Of hungers yet unlived,
Of Judas-words unsaid,
Deaths never to be shrived;
The fanatical procession
Of faiths in counter-strife,
Men's sanctified oppression
And vileness to each other.

All these lay there at rest
Upon our mother's breast,
Sharing the stream of life.

Mud

In war-years, long ago
My generation learned
To be afraid of mud.
We watched its vileness grow,
Deeper and deeper churned
From earth, spirit, and blood.

From earth, sweet-smelling enough
As moorland, field, and coast;
Firm beneath the corn,
Noble to the plough,
Purified by frost
Every winter morn.

From blood, the invisible river
Pulsing from the hearts
Of patient man and beast;
The healer and life-giver,
The union of parts,
The meaning of the feast.

From spirit, which is man
In triumphant mood;
Conqueror of fears,
Alchemist of pain
Changing bad to good;
Master of the spheres.

Earth, the king of space;
Blood, the king of time;
Spirit, their lord and god;
All tumbled from their place,
All trodden into slime,
All mingled into mud.

The Wartime Singers

It is time for us, the middle generation,
To stop singing.   The bells of our hearts are cracked.
Our throats when young were tortured, strained, and racked
With gun-fire, which we tried to sing above,
Like larks trilling their private, pathetic love
Above a forest-fire that sucked their nests.

We are dumb creatures who deserve veneration.
But the younger men coming, with proud, hard voices
Untainted by war, we cannot expect them
To pity the broken music within our breasts.
Why should we hinder the new-comer who rejoices
Over his new world, which he and his friends are raising
On the ruins we made?

      It is wise for us to pause,
To listen, to marvel at this young man's amazing
Effrontery, faith, in daring once more to build
A strange, hard music, compounded on different laws,
A symphony heedless of us, the broken and spilled,
The scrannel-piped scare-boys on the old battlefield.

PART EIGHT

THE SOLITARY MAN

1941

PART I

ONE WAR

France, 1940

TREADING frontier field and flowers
The dark invaders pass.
Dust rises, sky lowers,
Wheels bruise the grass.

Grief-huddled, sit and wait,
Nothing can be done.
Siege gathers at the gate;
Treachery blots the sun.

Who is the strongest here;
Singer or swordsman?
Let each lie cloaked in fear
Like snowbound herdsmen.

Fear is a fallow field;
Seeds lodge in despair.
You 'll see inaction yield
Strength unaware.

Yes, having plumbed the deep
Humiliation,
Sunk in a dreadful sleep,
Shamed man, shamed nation;

Suddenly renewed, the one
Arouses the other:
Dawn breaks, watchwords run
From brother to brother.

Loud shouts chanticlere,
Red-tasselled throat of brass;
Foes fall, skies clear,
Green springs the grass.

A Moment's Escape

A continent upon my back,
Heavy with threats of war,
Leaden with tyrannies,
I crept away from man.
I found a bridle-track
At dusk, heard the night-jar
Under monotonous skies
Shrunken thin and wan.

I knew that solitude enough
To ease bewilderment:
A yellow-hammer crying
Of noonday at day's end,
And the grim rooks' rough
Call from the firmament.
I forgot nations dying,
And Europe without a friend.

A House in Wartime

Look at this ancient house; it has survived
Three centuries of time, and human history.
Things have grown old in it.   Grandfather clocks
Have frayed much catgut hauling down the hours;
Pot handles have worn smooth, and poker-knobs
Been polished by palms long folded over breasts
Now quiet and untroubled in the churchyard.

Search any corner here, attic or cellar,
Odd pantry cupboard or a gunroom shelf,
You 'll find the throw-outs of ten generations,
Household rubbish made romantic by time;
Print bonnets, bundles of letters, broken toys,
Pathetic vestiges of civilized life,
Emblems of peace and a continued growth
In one place, in one faith, of civil man
And all his works.   Here is the centre of it,
That long activity in hope; the plans,
The achievement, the discarded and replaced,
All gathered in this house, beneath a roof
Where the bats hang, and hermit spiders lurk.

I should be sure enough of all I hold
Within such walls.   I should look out through windows
Set three feet back in mellowed brick and stone,
And stand secure amid my universe
Now turning to its rich, late summer days,
Life's discipline grown fruitful.   I should see,
Like some old patriarch in a lost religion,
My wife and children round me, the fulfilment
Of mutual love beyond the need of words.

Instead, I hear the wind wail in the walls.
By night and day I hear the fleets of death
Pass overhead, to deal out mutilation
On those who have no quarrel with the sky,
But look to it as their forefathers looked,
For rain, for sunshine, for the busy song
Of larks in spring, and movement of the stars,
Those symbols of a God half understood.

The ancient house dissolves.   My lifework thins
And a reverberation tears it down.
My gathered harvest is consumed in fire,
Thunder, and fire that flashes in their eyes,
My loved ones, gone down in their agony.
The raid is done.   The sky is clear again
For stars by night, and singing lark by day.
Eternity once more puts on the mask
Of time, to hide its dreadful wisdom from me.

Still, after peril, stands my house foursquare,
Still, with the nightmare passed, I may contrive
To comfort those I yet may call my own.
The clock ticks on, the bat and spider keep
A sacred shadow in the roof above.
Laughter, love's fullest echo, fills the house.
Nothing has changed, except that Universe
I dared to raise, before I looked on fear.

The Economist and the Poet

The Economist said to me: 'Let us go together
And watch the men and women of the ballet,
Those mortal fairies.'   But I shook my head.
'How can I come, whose mind cannot see whither
Europe is rushing, whether to blood and bullet,
Or to some other racial suicide
Of cornfields burnt, and machines laid aside,
None to buy their product, and an ape to sell it?
I, being concerned with words, find these grave matters
Tie up my thoughts, and put my verse in fetters.'

'Ah well,' he said, 'for many years I worried
On this and that expression of the verb,
Seeking a prose to suit the City Man.
I tried my sentences in every garb
The Masters recommended, but never one
Would fit my thoughts.   My paragraphs were horrid.'

'Yours is a simple problem,' I replied,
And he laughed too, echoing what I said.
And with that laughter, gay in our despair,
We took the extravagant and the wordless road
To watch the deathless creatures dance on air.

To-morrow

To-day in thought I came to a strange land
Whose people I was quick to recognize,
Whose tongue I instantly could understand.
A curious friendliness shone in their eyes,
And some in passing touched me by the hand,
Each gesture in its silence just as wise
As slow words most deliberately planned
By minds grown generous upon statesmanship.
It was an evening world.   I saw the sun,
Like a great harvest-wagon, westward dip,
While crowds walked after it, their labours done.
Then a man spoke, his scythe upon his shoulder,
'This is your blood-soaked world—but one day older!'

The Blind Surveyor

Compass and scale and ruler
Are useless in my hand.
I am a blind surveyor
Now I must measure love.

The distant hills that vanish,
The flower pressed in a book
And found by chance one evening
Beside an old-age fire;

The honeysuckle blossom
A boy plucked from a hedge
To match his mother's fragrant
And still unsilvered hair:

The sun and moon and planets
First worshipped by a youth
Yet innocent of closer
Torments of desire.

The dew upon all beauty,
And knowledge still in bud,
The faith in human nature,
A world untorn by war;

These I am told to measure
With memory, mind, and will;
What wonder that I falter,
And drop my tools, and weep?

Something Private

Waking this morning to a glory
Of birds and slant light in the orchard,
A mad diffusion of honeysuckle
On the air, and fields dew-hoary;
I rubbed my eyes with a sleepy knuckle,
Stung them to watchfulness, nurtured
On delight in the day.   I put behind
The sirens of the night, the terror
Of bombs, and children consumed with fire,
Deeds of pride and the evil mind,
By mothers' sons warped in the mirror
Of a madman's doctrine and desire.

Though knowing my post in the burning city,
My duty to neighbours in the street,
The need for team work rather than pity,
All heroics subdued and discreet,
With discipline so necessary and dull,
Still along my nerves I heard the feet
Of dancing life, and in my brain the pull
Of daydawn ideas, things to be done
Intimately, creation in private
Joy, engendered by the sun,
Then cast for all mankind to have it.

Riding up the Hill

Ride up the hill a little, and then turn
To look on the destruction.   You will see
Poor Shakespeare with a bullet in his throat,
And a scarred Cross, the relic of a Faith.

All will be silence in your solitude;
The last child dead, the mutilated woman
Huddled and motionless.   You knew that woman.
She was the mother of a million men.
A million more lie cheated in her womb.
She's fallen amongst the wild flowers, near the child,
The generation of spring, the fragrant carpet
Of hope, old earth's reassurance of life.

It will be best to hope.   You should stoop down
And pick a primrose splashed with human blood,
And set the symbol in your bandolier
Just where the tunic gapes above the wound,
The wounded mind that will for ever bleed,
For ever drain you of the power to love,
To cherish anything for more than a day.

That will not matter.   Your generation knows
The worst that can befall the race of man.
You have seen his work, his best; and you have seen
Poor Shakespeare with a bullet in his throat;
Your son, your mother flung into the dust;
All general glory and all private treasure
Tossed out, and trampled on, and done to death.

Ride on, my brother, still higher up the hill.
Then look again, and tell me what you see.

Secret Service

Here at the inn, become anonymous,
No longer the familiar bunch of keys
Burdens my pocket.   I have turned the locks,
Left the doors wide for those who care to search
In the old place, the lifetime lair.
                                        Farewell
To habit and to name.   I am called Pilgrim,
And travel is my habit.   I am restless,
Rootless, have surrendered my five senses,
And the possession of love, the confidence
Of marriage.   I am like the Jew, the sailor,
The man of service, the ever-questing man.

I have broken old bonds, sworn a new vow
To acknowledge no vow, to accept no duty.
My flight is irresponsible, I am free.
'Who are you?' asks the stranger at the inn,
The voice in the new city, voice on the road,
The wondering, wandering voice in the air I breathe,
The voice over the ruins of my old self, my world
That quaked and is broken, the house lying open
With the keys in the locks, and the doors flung wide.

'I am the guest,' I answer at the inn,
'The guest for a night; I am the rootless man,
I am the man without child, the man who has left
The pillow, the bosom, the protective arms
And the regenerative sleep at night.
I am the man with a ticket, a summons to go.
My place is in the corridors of life,
And I shall know for my caress the wind
At the corners of the world.
                                        Ever unknown,
Man of no service, man of no secrets, the man
Murdered one night at the inn, the anonymous man.'

The Solitary Man

Humbled by the large events
Of war, and all its needs,
I put away private intents
And personal greeds.

I button on the discipline,
My nation-coloured coat,
And take my station in the line,
Lost and remote.

Yes, I am lost, but well content;
Obscure, a cancelled soul,
To answer with the regiment
At the calling of the roll.

The roll-call!   I can hear it now
Ring round our threatened coast,
The challenge to the bully's blow,
The signal to the lost.

The lost of Europe!   For their sakes,
I and my British kind,
Freedom resign till freedom wakes
In each despairing mind.

For their sakes, and the others too,
The unborn of our race,
Whose right we in this act renew;
Our grace for their grace.

The Cycle

I know the truth!   For I have slept so long,
Slept through the troubled times, the rumbling wheels,
The iron caterpillars on the cornfields,
The loud rending apart of children's limbs,
The bomb competing with a woman's breasts.

Knowing these things were coming with the heroes,
I turned aside, hiding my head in fear,
And in that individual darkness saw
With a prophet's eye, the bomb before it fell,
The woman's breast still suckling the child,
The rosy limbs still kicking in her lap,
The green corn springing from untrodden soil.

Then, in mad imagination cloaked,
I saw the horror fall upon the world
Before it fell, taking my punishment
Before it came.   So through the deed I slept,
Bleeding from the uninflicted wound.

This is the quicker pulse of poet's blood;
To see the martyr in his mother's lap,
The crucified at play among the shavings,
The hero with the ball before the bomb
Poised in his fist.   And in that premature
Racing of the blood, the poet sees his death
Before he dies, and dies a thousand times
Though none beside himself has heard the wheels,
The iron caterpillars on the cornfields,
The loud rending apart of children's limbs,
The bomb competing with a woman's breasts.

Now all is over, I awake and find
The dream come true.   I see a shattered world;
The heroes, with their mischief pulled about them,
Lying buried in their own destruction.
The corn is springing green, another woman
Guides her warm nipple to the groping mouth,
And strokes the limbs still innocent of pain.
He who is first to fear, will be the first
To sing of fear's defeat, and joy returned.

The Unborn Historian

In these unmusical days I console myself
With the thought that, dark in a woman's womb
A mortal immortal, like the human race in its cave,
Lies waiting.   Or even that mother herself
Is unborn, and her mother, too, asleep, unconceived.

No matter! the singer is destined!   I hear
Centuries hence, perhaps, his wonder awaking;
I foresee his joy in the earth he believes is new,
His youth in a world that is young, the same that to us
Is old, crumbling, a ruin of passionate time.

He will cross this desert, he will find in this age of destruction
A motive for singing; he will see from the hills of the future
A landscape, a history, both simple, embalmed in the past,
And the song he will sing shall enshrine our despair,
Reveal our mad story, and from its present confusion
Discover the hope that guides us towards his birth.

PART II

ANOTHER WAR

Walking Alone

Back through the universal darkness, hands upon eyes,
I follow the path of prayer,
Stripping the action from old histories,
Layer after layer;
Casting them down to mark the road's return
Lest I should lose my way
In this dark journey where no beacons burn
Before the dawn of day,
The day of man, and his awakened brain,
His wheel of thought, spinning upon desire,
The swift direction to a wayward fire.

This shall be light enough.   There is no other.
Behind my hands, behind the lidded eyes
Heavy as ingots with the weight of thought,
I follow a gleam which none may smother,
No dust of earth, no star-dust from the skies,
No obscurations that false guides have brought
To-day, in my own life, or in the past
Of my long speculation over time,
Human disaster, the ruinous, vast
Occasions of mankind, base or sublime.

Poor traveller, alone with living,
I grope toward a way I cannot find,
Receiving nothing, and that nothing giving
Back through the humours of my mind,
Grim charity, and cold benevolence,
That love and minister to passing ghosts,
Marking them as a mockery of sense,
The sense of time and all its vanished hosts.

Yes, I pass them on my way;
But as a woodman through a forest passes
The pressing foliage, leaves numberless,
A multitude that makes the light of day
Something beyond and unbelievable:

Or as a tiger through the tropical grasses
Shouldering past each pollen-heavy tress
And spilling a million seeds.
So I through other centuries, and deeds
Innumerable and fruitful as the grass,
Urged by my hunger, pass.

The thinking mind is like that beast of prey.
It kills for joy and drinks the active blood.
It has no scruple for the world it treads,
But murders as it goes, and does not stay;
Following where its icy passion leads,
Ignoring present deeds half understood,
Intent on those of yesterday,
The lights, the sounds,
The dead flesh and the congealing wounds.

Who is this monster within me, that dissembles
Prayer, and studies humility?
What is its purpose under the warm sky
Of the world, where the fruitful raincloud tumbles
And stirs the earthy odours, the must,
The humus, the fur, the velvet skin,
The innocent clinging and the forms of lust
That clasp, and bring forth life, and know no sin.

But thought is sterile, pure and cold.
It hunts alone, and has a virgin greed
Not of this world.   Its hunger is old,
More ancient than creation, before earth,
God's seventh day; before his first
Woke, conscious of primeval thirst,
And in a self-contorting motion
Of anger in the loins of mirth,
Created all that future life should need,
Heaving and fertile ocean.

But thought looks out upon the sea, and knows
Itself more ancient, more unsatisfied.
It does not dread the storm, the swollen tide.
Thought, with its feather-blows,
Opens what nature never shall divide.
It seeks the very presence, then will dare
To touch the wounded hands, the wounded side,
And after its cold ecstasy of prayer,
Lift the dead eyelid from the dying eye,
And whisper to the God, 'Thou shalt not die!'

The Wrong Road

Say this when you return,
'I came by the wrong road
And saw the starved woods burn.
I stopped, bewildered, lost,
And of a sudden, heard
The red-throated bird,
The holy bird, the ghost.
I felt the shivering reed
Fevered with frost.
I watched the Crucified
Writhing upon the Cross
With the spear in His side,
And beneath him the moss
With the crimson buds
Tortured, multiplied
Under the dripping goad,
Close by the road,
The wrong road.'

The Last Revolution

The winter sunshine on parade
Draws its cold steel, and raises
A distant cheer on the horizon.
The ageing heart knows what that praise is;
Recognizing the revolution
With the grey flag, the quiet voice,
The final preparations made
For the coming kingdom of frost,
Where hopes are withered into beauty
And loss is worth all that is lost:
While down the twig-ends of desire,
Drop after drop, icicles form
A parody of former fire,
A poetry of the past storm.

Only the old will be content
To thaw their waning strength for this
Last gesture, and rouse their minds to make
This frigid sculpture of a kiss,
Knowing the fever of their past
Is permanent at last.

Two Ways

Some are afraid of Death.
They run from him, and cry
Aloud, shrinking with fear
When he draws near.
Others take their last breath
As though it were a sigh
Of sheer content, or bliss
Beneath a lover's kiss.
Perhaps it is not much,
After life's labour,
That summoning touch
Of Death, our neighbour.

The Word

Now, returning to idleness,
Comes the true labour.
With step slowed, and mind languid,
To attend the flowering word,
To linger over syllable sepals
Unfolding, revealing the core
And the seed of wisdom.

A man of affairs,
Bound by a thousand duties,
Writing, debating, ordering,
I was lost in the noise,
The loud rotation of phrase;
The empty clatter of words.

Now, in my idleness,
Under a silence
Wide as the dome of midnight,
One word appears, like a star.

The flower: the star:
The creatures of air and of space,
The perfume so near, the light from afar,
The distilling of thought,
The newly discovered,
The word!

The Martyr

Death is not more terrible than this
Stillness in the heart,
Silence in the mind!
Unfeeling, unthinking; no kiss,
No image, no ecstasy or hurt;
Only this waiting like a lull of wind
Between a fall of snow and a fall of snow
There is nothing fear may not know;
But knowledge is the scar of an old wound.

Fettered with the past,
And with the future bound,
Dreading the moment that cannot last,
Mankind, Sebastian, shot
With these arrows, all three
Pinning him through to the tree;
Such is his lot.

But yesterday, to-day, to-morrow,
His triple torture, he loves them still.
For them he lives a sainthood of his own,
Nourishing hope upon a feast of sorrow
And virtue on the last defeat of will.
Even when hope is gone,
And all he hears is the echo of his moan,
Still he strains at the bond and the mesh,
Tearing his wounds afresh,
Plucking the arrows from his shuddering flesh,
Straining and rending the roots of the tree,
And crying aloud, 'I am free!'

The Dear Ghost

What!   You disturb me again?   You should be sleeping:
Asleep, I say, not roving the world of men,
Treading the air so gravely with never a word,
Or none that fleshly ear has ever heard;
Treading the air between the now and then
Of time, divisions meaningless to you.

Is it like that the other side of death:
No rock to rest on, and no road for keeping
A chosen course; no roses, and no dew
To add to their temptation?   What is your food,
What sins are yours, what takes the place of lust
In lands where nothing or nobody is begotten,
And there is no decay, dust unto dust?

Or is it charnal there; even knowledge rotten,
Mathematics tasting flat in the mouth,
And music tumbled to a monotone?
Is the compass closed, north made one with south,
East met with west, and all strange customs gone?
Is it a commune there, which you have left
Because of its perfection?   Do you crave
For the five senses once again, the deft
Turn of delight, forbidden by the grave?

O brother, once with living, nervous fingers
Making such fugal patterns out of sound
That brain and heart of living men resolved
Into unmeaning unity of grief
That rang like joy upon this stony ground
And broke it into elements, and delved
To find their master at earth's centre—iron,
And ring a summons that to this moment lingers;
Oh, brother, that is done!   Those fingers now
Flutter unfleshed, without the blood's attire on
To give them weight, a mind's significance.

What mind is that?   The mind I knew?   The mind
You nurtured on the various evidence
Of sight, sound, touch, a woman's hair
Stirred by your breath, that messenger of speech?

Has love such instruments to serve it there
Between the worlds, out of our sensual reach?
If I should follow you, what should I find,
The same, where none are alike, none different?
You knew no more than I before you went.
Do you know now, or is no knowledge there
In the realm you wander out of, into again
Without volition, with no glad mysteries
Shining from the sockets that once were eyes?
Is it like this; and have you died in vain?

Uneasy Marriage

One day nearer, one day in advance
Of the earlier dread, the illusory tread,
Tread of the years, with the bell-stroke of winter,
The iron ringing of frost; the following trance
Of the narcissus lost where its perfumes enter
The pond edge, and madden the water with longing;
One day nearer the summer, the bruising of grass
Under love, and the nightingales' empty singing
With wonder and sleep, and a horror that will not pass;
One day nearer the autumn, with the manly work,
The farewell to love, the turn to political fruit,
As the tree sheds wealth, each leaf with its mark
Of gold, and decay in close pursuit.

That is the tale of a day.   Is it enough
To round off a life, to snatch it from time
And testify to the soul's immortal stuff
Whose season is yet single and sublime?

Or must the folly of the four divisions
Fail with their heat and cold, their love and loss,
Leaving us strangers where we most inherit
And foreign to the seed that we have spilled
Careless of need, and ignorant of merit,
While the rash act an unknown self has willed
Overtakes knowledge, grows ominous and gross,
And plays the tyrant until death has stilled
The uneasy marriage under stones, and filled
Their intervals with counterfeiting moss?

Atlantis

Where Atlantis lies
In the waters of the west,
Love turns longing eyes,
Mourning what is lost.

For though Love may be blest,
And take the joy he craves;
In taking, he has lost
Atlantis under the waves.

The Man without Faith

A man without faith
Grows old before his years,
His world a wraith,
For whom the end nears
Like a winter mist
When the sun is cold
In the cold west.

His children about him
Are strangers, unknown.
The love that begot them
Cooled and gone.
If he get riches
They turn to rust,
And he can do nothing
With a handful of dust.
Life's miracle fails him,
Life's rapture, life's breath;
He has done with living,
He has forestalled death.

The Eleventh Brother

There is one brother still,
Whose arm is a swan's wing.
His fate I 'll not forget;
Maimed by the stroke of time,
The moment short, the sting
Of the nettle-woven shirt.

And then, through no man's will,
Because of no man's crime,
Doomed for ever, his lot
A semi-human farce,
A hand-and-feather game.

Even his prayer for grace,
With pinion pressed to palm,
While the words wait unsaid,
Discovers a grimace
Of smothered mirth from God.

Hemlock in Hand

Wait! before you drink despair!
Set down the cup a moment, pause
To think of what you leave;
And then—but this is if you dare—
Consider where you go, the cause
That is the end as well.

Will you take the cup again,
After that foretaste of hell:
Or will the vision cancel pain,
Love derided, wealth fooled away,
Studious years lost in a day,
And, worst treachery of all,
The self-betrayal of the soul?

You will not find oblivion worth
Even these miseries lost.
Time like a curtain torn, earth
Ploughed and then left fallow,
Rivers with no sea to follow,
And every human face a ghost;
Even these are certain, flown
Though light may be out of them,
There is still no doubt of them.
But the other, waiting on the cup,
Lurking as you drink it up,
Ah!   That is utterly unknown!

The Final Gift

A man grown weary of his greed
Turns from the chink of coin,
And the perpetual need
Of his clamorous loin.
He finds music enough,
And the sky's grace above;
Such gossamer stuff
As the nightingale's love,
Or a pause on the road
To ease a man's load.
Nothing more of his own
Is worth a hand's lift;
His passion has flown,
He has won life's last gift.

The Friends

These men, now both alert and watching
With mental rapiers unbuttoned,
Blade to blade, nerve-tautened, touching
In contact of caressing hate,
Were lately friends.   They have not broken
Faith; the unvowed vows are tightened,
And neither deems himself forsaken.
Yet now they face each other, stand
With steely judgment in right hand,
Feeling through this cold medium
The death they know dare not deny them.

Unseen the fantasy has risen,
The mist upon a shining day,
Bringing decay and light's corrosion.
Such is the brain's uneasy way,
Confronted, failing to understand
The unscrupulous logic of the heart.

With mutual state now undermined,
Both in their hatred loving more,
Each knows, in playing his murderous part,
The duel is doubly civil war.

The Hero

I could tell you of a young man
Blown with heroism into Spain.
He had a knapsack of philosophy,
And as he went he scattered the small grain
Of his few songs under the dangerous sky.

A girl, grown fond, thought him too young to die.
She put the memory of their secret joy
Behind her heart, and turned to public deeds,
Neglecting the earth he trod, and his scattered seeds.

But soon she was brought to child-bed, with a boy
Smiling up at her as his father had smiled.
And thankfully she saw that his plump back
Carried no philosophic haversack.
She saw, too, that his lips displayed no zest
For song, but only for his mother's breast.
That being so, she found she could forgive
The man who died so that a dream might live,
And faith with prudence remain unreconciled.

The Eavesdropper

Not much is known about him since he died.
I watched the girl who stood above his grave
And heard the sound upon his coffin, heard
A woman weeping over the dusty word,
The epilogue a stranger always speaks.

Sometimes it is not useful to be brave.
That girl was overlooked.   In a way, she lied
By standing so demurely, near another's grief.
But I saw her seeking as an animal seeks
Somewhere in secret to bleed its broken life
Away.   The other woman was his wife.
Hers were the tears that bring their own relief.

But this one, whom I spied on to my shame,
Did not even envy that despair.
I saw her flinch, force herself to stare
At nothing; then go as quietly as she came.

I wondered what she left beside him there.

Grief's Reflection

In the Cretan winding of the brain,
Finding my way by the dropped thread
From the present world driven insane
To the sanity of the dead,
I grew callous toward the slain,
The millions mutilated,
The maimed children of China and Spain,
Fugitive, stricken dumb,
And the generation to come
Warped in the womb.

I turned from this reality
And looked in Ariadne's loom,
Map of the labyrinth, the grey
Corridors of time and thought
Where the past looks like the Bull.

And what I saw was beautiful;
An old death, a brother dying,
His music at that moment wrought
And frozen, and falling silently,
Snowy sound, and the storm done,
Covering a vanished day,
For a white eternity
Settled there, for ever lying.

What might this be, I wondered,
Since no man might condone
My craven flight into the past,
The responsibility pondered
And dropped, the retreat alone,
The seeking of a private grief
In the brain's labyrinthine path,
Snatching therefrom some relief
From to-day's universal wrath?

But there's no answer! No, none!
The gentle loss, the musician dying,
Holding a brother's hand, my hand,
Sweet life resigning with a sigh;
All this, forgotten for so long
Or recalled like an old song,
Is now a stabbing agony!
And in response I have lost sight
Of our immediate grief, the lost
Millions in this European night
Of tyranny and holocaust.

Be Frugal

Be frugal in the gift of love,
Lest you should kindle in return
Love like your own, that may survive
Long after yours has ceased to burn.

For in life's later years you may
Meet with the ghost of what you woke
And shattered at a second stroke.
God help you on that fatal day.

Meeting with you, and walking by your side,
First as a stranger quiet with admiration,
As people will, when a journey looms ahead
And self is lost in the exciting sense of travel,
I looked from time to time, shyly and hidden,
And saw a person dangerous to my peace;
A gipsy beauty with the passion stilled
Into a watchful laughter, content to wait
Upon events, for judgment of a man.

But later, on the way, some boldness crept
Into the chance companionship, and chance
To fate was changed.   Destiny took charge.
At once the journey livened, I forgot
The cause for setting out, forgot the goal,
And found myself praying to travel on,
For ever with this stranger by my side,
Praying so fervently that I looked again,
Curious to discover more about you,
Disturber and delight.   Looking again,
I saw myself reflected in your kindness.
Ah, quietude within a woman's mind,
Fountain of patience where a man may come
To quench his thirst after the salt of learning
And fire of poetry have seared his throat!

Travel, they say, discovers character,
Flexes the firmest muscles of the mind,
And tests all beauty by the bone beneath.
So found I on that journey.   What you found
I shall not question.   All I know is this;
The road, the weariness, the front of time
Were servants to our joy, giving it strength,
Not sapping it; and when the dark came down
We drew together, closer by the bridge,
Paused while I asked, and while you gave assent.
Then in sweet agony we crossed the bridge.

South Pole

There 's no reversal now,
Our shadows point the way,
Into the virgin snow,
Into the endless day.

Here at the Southern Pole
We bear the globe, and feel
The burden of the whole,
And know it is not real.

Ocean and continent,
The race of beast and man,
Have shrunk into a point
That turns on a glove-span.

We know that where we stand,
The equatorial wars
Still rage, but in our hand,
Small as the southern stars.

Atlas, who shouldered Earth,
Knew less than we know now;
He sponsored mankind's birth:
We are silent in the snow.

A Mystery

Is there a deeper mystery than this;
The still air, the still heart,
The meeting of memory and time
Before the abyss;
The faith that will let lovers part
After long life together;
The knowledge in darkness, the hand
Invisible, the foothold
Where no foot may stand,
The voice on the mountain
Defying the height and the cold?

A Nocturne

Only this left-hand turning; only this folly,
To take the side street into yesterday
Where a garden of regret and melancholy
Invites too easily.   The other way
Should be my way, the straight road with traffic
And jolting elbows to remind me of it,
To make the present real, the future graphic.

But I can smell white lilac, see the curds
On the bush, immaculate, sunlit or moonlit.
And I can hear a dying woman's words
Reproaching someone whom I dare not name.
Who are they now, who were they in those days
Before experience and understanding?
What dramatist was at work, recording shame,
Courting an unseen audience's praise
With dialogue whose grieving rhythms ring
Still through the garden, in that scented night?

And were they truly overheard by one
Who still survives, to dream, and turn aside
From so-called sanity and sufficient grace
Of action, everyday delight and fear?
What is the guarantee of dreams?   They run
Their measured course like comets, and as they glide,
Their incandescence brings illusion near,
Conjuring again the time, the place,
With every dreadful motive doubly clear,
But now so fruitless, as the vision burns
Out in the dark, and blinding day returns.

PART III

SURVIVALS

The Warmonger

THAT thrush is getting anxious.
What's he worried about?
He's been nagging all the morning
With his triple shout.
Every time I lift my spade
I hear him upbraid
Another bird I cannot see,
Like a man who yells to hide
That he's more than half afraid
Of gardeners peaceable as me.

Archaeology

They say a church once stood in this Anglian field.
But there's no village here it could have served.
The district is a plateau, wide and wild
Where winds meet, and scrub-bush only has thrived
For centuries, except on one lonely farm.

Here in its acres set grim and taciturn,
An outpost of humanity, it holds
Authority of a field or two; no more.
The wind is master here, and grudgingly yields
A yearly crop of corn, too thin for flour.

But in the early summer, when the tyrant
Relents for a month, and growing lenient
Breaks into bramble-flowers, and eglantine,
And all the little outlaws man dismisses
From garden beds and honestly hoed fields,
Then the dim murmurs of old homes, and guesses
About a church once sanctifying these wilds,
Are proved in barley. Where it rises green
A deeper hue of tall blades, cruciform,
Reveals the old foundations. No need to search
By gossip or legend. There stands the living church.

Be Patient

Deeds up to date are bad enough;
A topical man runs mad.
I should prefer to ponder things
I formerly had.

A sin forgotten is a sin
Repented of and salved.
Evil, by process of neglect,
Is halved.

Think, if a woman troubled you,
And tore you, shred by shred,
Would you not curse her beauty,
Wish yourself dead?

But such a curse were premature;
You 'd but need to wait,
And time would set her loveliness
Beyond love, or hate.

And think again, if an armed man
Shall desecrate your house,
In a few years that noise will sound
Like a foraging mouse.

Charred passion, and a broken wall,
Make ruins that will lean
With more significance than the unrifled
Originals now mean.

The Inept

Go where you will,
Whatever you touch,
You, being the odd chick of the clutch,
Are doomed for ever to climb the hill,
To fumble, and spill
The essence that wiser men shall distil,
To wander, meet smug folk, and great,
Reducing them all to your own half-state,
Confusing the fool with his folly,
The song and the singer,
The blood with the bone.
And when you should be gone, cleanly and wholly,
You will linger!

Winter Sunshine

In mid-December by a southern wall
I sat and heard the midges wake and drone
Making a moment's summer of their own
Before the steaming bricks.   I heard the call
Of a deluded thrush, whose triple fall
Lulled me like scent of roses long since blown.
I saw an ant return, seeking alone
To drag a cocoon from its winter stall.

Content with these small signs, I then decided
To shrink my large ambitions, hopes and plans,
Such as are normally a healthy man's
Whose life with work and play is well divided,
And make this miniature perfection be,
With ant, and midge, and thrush, enough for me.

The Nuptials

This chance encounter in the street,
Satirized by a million elbows
Prodding our shyness as we meet,
Is yet enough; for instinct knows
More than the clumsy lips can say.
It watches in this tumult, blows
Metropolis like gossamer away,
Surrounds us with windless air,
Makes us impervious, and then
Invisible to men.

Therefore unseeing, and unseen,
We can afford to give
All that has ever been
Lavished in exchange of love;
Without shame in word, or glance,
Or the withdrawn, untouching touch,
We have been mated in this chance
Encounter in the street.   Now each
May break the spell, and leave
The other, as the crowds move,
Fulfilled, vanishing.

The Revolution

'I am bowed down to earth with other men's words!
See!   My hand trembles with the stress of thought;
Nor can I lift the load of memory.
Surely the time has come to hear the birds,
To find delight that logic has not wrought;
To recall nothing under the open sky?'

So cried the revolutionary man,
Pale in his book-lined room, blinking, peering,
Holding a frightened hand to his deaf ear.

Then suddenly the crimson urchins ran
Along his veins, and stormed his heart with cheering
And flushed his brain to make his senses clear.

Spring in Town

From the spike on the town-bough,
Tipped with country fire,
I have instinct enough
To acknowledge desire;
To lift my head, to snuff
The odorous south,
And kiss the Invisible
Upon her mouth.

Old mischief once more
Prompts blood, and assails
The reasonable brain.
My mad vision feels
Catkin, leaf, flower,
And lost years again.

I would ask of the air
And dissembling sky,
What satire is this,
That the future seems fair,
And mature wisdom dare
Cherish the lie
Of that barmecide kiss?

The Month of March

In days when limbs drag
And the soul is sick,
It is good to see green leaves
Spring, flag upon flag,
On the glistening branches,
While crocuses prick
The soil, perfumes rise,
Blackthorn blanches,
The thrush performs
His triple trick,
From throat ruffled and dirty:
The blackbird, still
Songless, lances
Shower-charmed worms
With his yellow bill:
And the sun at six-thirty
Rises over the hill.

Narcissus

Close your eyes, and hooded thus,
Gaze up and inward to your brain.
What do you see, a universe
As ordered and as plain
As the spiral of the suns
With the motion of their fires,
Their mathematical desires—
Or do you see a dunce?

I pray it be the latter vision.
A man who looks within
And stumbles on a universe,
Is victim of a curse,
That coils, all serpentine with sin,
And drugs him with the old illusion!
He will dream of the Eagle's wing,
As did Roman consuls once,
And will crown himself a king—
Unless he be a dunce!

The Hours of a Day

I planted twelve green acorns in the sun,
Another twelve I set in the light of the moon.
Thinking then that the whole task was done,
I believed that I should be rewarded soon.

Nodding in that faith, I fell asleep
Through many generations of living and dying,
Sinking into solitude so deep
That even dreams lost their fertility.

Such was my reward.   When I awoke
I looked for stars, but something hid the sky.
I listened for peace, but a million leaves were sighing
Over my head, oak interlocked with oak!

Small Mercies, 1934

Three years have gone since I looked down
From ridge of rock and snow
To Freiburg jewelled on the plain
Four thousand feet below.

But I can smell the icy air,
And hear my voice ring out
With mountain clearness like a flame
That time still blows about.

If sight, sound, smell can thus survive
Thought's slow, corrosive greed,
I'll keep my faith in senses five,
And scorn a greater need.

Joy

Grief is articulate, but joy
Is a dumb-founded boy.
He stands in the grass, in the wind,
Aware of the ocean before him,
Aware of the mountains behind,
And the way of the sky, the way
Of the earth, and the wonders of both.
But to speak of these things he is loth;
He is dumb, he has nothing to say.

Joy in the Making

Longing for rhyme and measure, and the beat
Of sleepy verses stumbling to their feet,
Fortune attended him that dancing day.
The poet watched the virgin at her play,
Waiting his time, and hers, knowing she saw
His swift intention to destroy the law,
And with it, the chastity she wearied of.

No song is made without release of love
And something fiercer that attacks the womb
And sets therein a miniature of doom,
A fate of words.   The maidenhead knew this,
And looked towards the poet for a kiss
That would consume her limbs, and shake her mind
With love's loud knocking summons fast behind
The breath, the thrust, the blindness and the bright
Aftermath of intolerable light.

It was not she, but he, whose latent fears
Bred verses with harelip and asses' ears.

Late Love

Love coming late, comes like an autumn sun
Upon a field of corn delayed by drought.
It breathes a ripeness we must do without,
Foreseeing frost with harvest just begun,
And all our hopes like swallows, one by one
Assembling but for flight and winter rout,
Winged affirmations circling round about
Our fragile sky, then suddenly gathered and gone.

But being wise, knowing our poverty,
What meagre years we have to give each other,
We make a richness of it.   Time may smother
Our fire too soon—already in the sky
Light droops westward—yet even so, we wait
In peace the starlight aftermath of fate.

Father of flowers and trees,
Look on my shining spade.
It has just planted these
Next-year promises
In the garden I have made.

Cut from a fallow field,
Hedged against the wind,
I 'll swear to make it yield
Beauty to your mind.

I offer you my sweat,
Labour of muscle and brain.
Come then, with generous heat,
And summer gifts of rain.

What you give, I will take,
Repaying by my toil
With fork, and hoe, and rake
Your promise to my soil.

Reading in a Field

Suddenly to become magnificent,
Gold in one hand, in the other an apple
From the tree forbidden to the innocent,
And on the Mediterranean hardly a ripple:
That is the dream coming suddenly over a book
Where I sit reading in the English sun.
I dare to read no more; I dare not look
Beyond the page for fear the glories run
Into the present, like water into sand,
Leaving my mind to thirst before a mirage
Upon the desert of time.   I close my hand
On common herbs, buttercup and borage;
The gold of Greece, the fruitfulness of Rome
Conjured and lost again, in sight of home.

Revolt

The interminable structure of words
Occupies a poet's life.
He grows old, grows blind,
Loses reality, goes secretly mad,
Scorns the easy singing of the birds,
Preferring the music of his weary mind,
Confusing thus the joyous with the sad,
And peace with strife.

Why should he adulterate his heart
With reason, and cloud his sense
Thereby?   Let the wise fool
Forget his shrewd grammarian's part,
And all the subtle science of the tense,
Learning to live and sing by rule
Of chance, the other man's wife!

Buying Fuel

Now I come to the farmer about some logs.
He says in a casual way, 'You can have pear.'
I stare at him for a moment.   Shall I dare
Tell him I know that on the smithied dogs
In the brick hearth, black oakwood soaked in bogs,
Rose-roots, apple, ash with its swift, short flare,
And sparks thrown chimney-length to the open air,
Or elm that looks the part but easily clogs,
No firewood smells like pear?   My conscience jogs
Me, saying, 'Tell him that it isn't fair.'

And so I do.   But he just laughs and looks,
Thinking I'm crazy.   'I don't charge for smells,'
He says, 'only for labour and the wood.
I'll bet you got that notion out of books.'
But he is wrong; such perfume with its spells
Has never been described nor understood.

233

Drought

In the brittle season of drought
Between the rain of spring
And the coming winter's flood,
We have learned to do without
Hedgerow flower, and flitting wing.
But we hear the cuckoo's shout,
Telling a story of mixed blood
With nothing prudent, and no shame
For confusion of a name.

In the dry season, with the sun
Making strict and lofty course
Daily through a heaven of light,
We have learned to wait on one
Pure and elemental force
Out of aspiration spun
By our spirits making flight
Far from earth.   But still we hear
Cuckoo! Cuckoo! through the year.

A Gardener's Farewell

It is the last evening here.
Farewell to house and garden,
The bushes we know,
The beech tree, our warden,
Sheltering all that is dear
To a gardener's heart, the slow
And unwilling to grow,
But the most lovely at last.
Farewell to those.

The sky fades.   Clouds close
Sadly over the west.
We will go into the house, turn
Away from all this, the shade
Of the evening tree, the still
Lamps lit in the flowers, that burn
With a fire stored up from the sun
Now day is done.

Summer Labour

Where lilac sleeps in the sun,
And dusty sparrows dream,
I warm my frosty fingers,
And feel the blood grow fluid,
Returning to my brain
With thoughtful bloom, and perfume
Essential from the earth.

Though still my humour lingers
With winter and the rain
Whose sterilizing rigour
Bound mood and beast and blossom,
I hear the cuckoo's mirth,
And know work must be done.

Seeking the Island

Now my life's journey has passed the high places,
I know, having looked out over the water,
The ocean where the western island was,
That I shall never see its palaces,
Its golden walls where the wise men sit
Heavy with their memory of race, memory deeper
Than reason, the men who never grow old.

But maybe this certainty of losses,
Of time's treachery in lacking hereafter,
The island, where the fountain of knowledge was,
Sunk in the ordinary waves, the terraces
And serene canals no longer lit
With the world's young light, maybe I, the sleeper,
Have reached there, awakened, and shall never grow old.

PART NINE

THE PORTRAIT OF THE ABBOT

1926

THE PORTRAIT OF THE ABBOT

HERE is the story of a certain monk
Whose fear of heaven shut him up for life
Within tall bell-reverberating walls,
Though all he loved and longed for was without.
He loved the simple things of life; the shapes
Of clouds hulldown along the eastern sky,
With evening splendour glowing in their sails.
When the cold summons of the Matins rang,
He'd wake, and follow with his silent brethren:
But the damp pavements which he gazed upon
Were pencilled with the contour of the hills,
And petal forms were shaped upon the dark.
That far-set light toward which we goad our thoughts
Through the dim mansion of our inward sight
When with fierce hands we press our lidded eyes
To shut the dissipating world away,
Even that gleam, the distant form of God,
His wanton fancy played with, changing it
To mundane shapes of human filigree.
He groaned upon the blasphemy, and moaned
Between the treacherous fingers which refused
To hold that wandering vision of the mind
Centred upon the singleness of God.

The hours of cloistral meditation brought
No ease from that rebellion of the eyes:
For did a gleam of sunlight fall on moss,
Or burnish some small lichen in the stone,
He straightway lost the thread of contemplation,
And all the traffic of the soul became
Removed and shadowlike behind the loud
Immediate clangour and the colour of sense.
He called himself a villain for these whims,
And lashed himself with solitary pains
Inflicted by the thongs that conscience knots.
He vowed to subjugate himself, and planned
Such schemes of deep contrition as subdued
His very soul with misery.   'Tis said
That he was found within his cell one day
Prepared with needle and with brazier
To plunge those guilty eyes into their hell
Of everlasting darkness.   But the deed

Was held suspended as he gazed in awe
Upon the graceful flames that leaped and changed
With such divine invention that they seemed
Praise-giving sprites, not forerunners of hell.

Colour he learned to dread.   It mastered him;
Called with bewitching cries and throat-laughter;
Took shape, and beckoned him with woodland hands
Ever luring, ever vanishing
Along those forest aisles where shadow hovers
Above the litter where the Seven lie,
The wayward darlings of the sun and earth.

Day after day with their relentless joy
The little things of beauty bore him down.
He dared not look upon the cobbled path,
For there were shapes, and such interstices
As held a myriad changes of delight.
And night brought no cessation; for his brain,
Sharpened by guiltiness, had gleaned from day
A store of loveliness to dream upon.

Then from that passion sprang the furtive habit
Which stealthily gained more tenacious power,
Persuading him with gifts; of skilful hand,
And surer vision.   He found himself at last
Perpetuating aims of vagary
By giving form to fanciful deceits
That lured him from the adoration of God,
The single, central object life should hold.

Kneeling upon the cold refectory flags
He 'd find himself with scouring-stone in hand,
Tracing the outline of a flying heron,
Who rose above the waters by the mill,
Spreading her wings like worship to the sky.
There upon the flagstone, limned in faint
And fading grey upon the colder grey,
The splendid creature soared with pinions wide.
Then for a moment, proud of his creation,
He 'd kneel, and look upon his handiwork,
Until some footfall woke him from his trance
And branded him defeated once again.
Ah! with what gesture of despair he leaned
Above those precious sins, and scoured them out!

   So rolled the bitter struggle year by year,
Until at last, with fortitude outworn,

And in his soul the artist's passion triumphant,
He called upon authority for aid,
And such external discipline as lay
Within the Abbot's rule.   'Father,' he cried,
'Protect me from myself.   The time has come
When all my harsh defences are thrown down
By this unanswerable eloquence of skill.
See how these treacherous hands are guiding me
Toward the gauds and vanities of the world.
My sinful eyes must worship what they see.
Save me from sight, my Father; blind my eyes,
So that by seeing nothing, I may see
What matters most, the countenance of God.'
'Shall you behold that?' was the calm reply.
'Then you indeed were blessed above all men.
Beware lest your contrition be too fierce.
There is a penitence of wilfulness.
God, who makes us all, made you, my son.
The subtle hands that you cry out upon
Are His designing.   Is it blasphemy,
I wonder, to deny their strength and skill,
And starve them of their fitting avocation,
The praise, by imitation, of God's craft?
But conscience, that inscrutable mystery,
Must be obeyed, though reason urge us on.
Therefore—and may it be God's will that guides me—
I now decide that you must paint no more.
Earth's beauties overwhelm you, chain your mind
In idle moods that may be Devil's drug:
What might be your salvation is your bane.
But, for a test of strength, find this respite.
Upon my death you shall take up the brush
And picture my successor.   If you live
Beyond his tenure, you shall paint again,
And set beside your former masterpiece
Another to enrich our eyeless walls.
But—now by your confession be you judged—
No other shall you paint; no woman's grace,
No fragile wing, no ringlet of a child,
No springtime blossom.   It is your own decree,
Dictated by your conscience, who, enthroned
Within the soul, administers your life
According to the whispered word of God.
I grieve for you, my brother.   Be it so.'

241

Time, with its assuaging waters, flowed
Year after year past those monastic walls.
The noon upon the morning with its bells
Followed with sober bells.   And prayer and chant,
Meditation, dormitory talk,
Garden cares, and charitable deeds;
Such was the fabric of the holy life.
Then evening with its noise of homing rooks;
With falling light on elm trees and flushed towers,
And, president of sound, the brooding bells.
So passed the years; and slowly old temptation
Floated like mountain foam along the stream,
Bubble by bubble with their rainbow hues
Vanishing, until at last the stream
Forgot its youth of hillside turbulence,
And flowed serene towards oblivion.

So peace came to the monk: the harsh division
And inward treachery were covered up.
No more could heron's flight before his eyes
Light them with sudden ecstasy, that threw
His soul into a tumult, and disturbed
The pool of contemplation there, which held
The image of a heaven far above.
No ample-bosomed tree asleep at noon
Within the drowsy meadows, where the light
Hangs gnatlike, shuddering at whiles:
No trooping cattle, with slow, serene pace
Following home, their westward-gleaming flanks
Rolling like laden ships upon the sea:
No heights, with snowy isolation capped,
Standing unmoved above the winter sun,
Until, his ardour fading, they return
An icy gleam, a rose of recognition:
No pebble, by a sudden vein of quartz
Inspired with lightning-shaped and jagged beauty:
None of these clayey splendours moved him now.
Habit, with careful method, year by year
Settled the dust of routine on his heart
And hid the fingerprints of clutching Joy,
Who used to hold him, killing breath with bliss.
Closer over the affairs of God he stooped;
Lower to sombre tasks he dragged his mind;
Schooling himself with such monastic duties
As made him reverenced in the brotherhood.

The aging Abbot year by year deputed
Power of administration to his hand,
Until the hours of solitude became
So few, that he grew clumsy in their use,
And squandered them in timid restlessness,
Half tinged with dread; such as a woman feels
Who sees, by chance, an old neglected portrait
That once she kissed in sullen agony,
With lips still virginal, yet half betrayed.

At last, the Abbot, wearing the thin flesh
Lighter and lighter on his boyhood soul,
Knew that his hour was come to stand revealed
In naked strength, and join the Sons of Morning.
But, ere relinquishing that earthly shift,
Hugging it round him to disguise his joy,
He called his friend, and clasped him close, and whispered:
'I am the only one who knows your pain.
And now I go, and leave you quite alone.
But where I go, I shall not be a stranger,
For I have seen already, here on earth,
The soul triumphant. Heaven holds no more.
Bravely you fought, and my decree was harsh.
But since your conscience craved it from my lips,
I did my duty, and the will of God.
Tell me, has your right hand forgot its cunning?
For my successor now will soon be here.'

The reverent brothers laid him in the tomb,
And burned their candles for the pious dead.
But still no answer dared the monk's white lips
Breathe to his wounded soul. Four days he knelt.
The quiet monastery was hushed with awe,
And seemed to shrink about the huddled figure,
Just as a mother over her anguished child
With fierce-eyed tenderness will hover close,
Jealous of her exclusion by such grief.
The monks, flitting like shadows to and fro,
Would pause with dumb inquiry, but not dare
To touch him, nor to move the beaker close,
Though bread nor water had not passed his lips
Since there he knelt to that unnatural strife
Within the cruel silence of the mind,
Upon those bloodless and untrampled fields
Where self meets self, and hate and love encounter
In fratricidal passion, cold and stern.

243

None knew his grief.   They thought he grieved, indeed,
For all the sweet and mutual intercourse
Which day by day, and year by year, had flowed
Like tidal waters through the two men's hearts,
Until their thoughts, and deeds, and loves were mingled;
Divided only when they turned to prayer,
Though maybe, even then, so near to God,
Each felt some tingling warmth within his breast:
A gleam of brotherly joy, pulsing and glowing,
A cottage lamp beneath the august stars,
A mortal nearness under lonely heaven.

They whispered how the two had worked together,
Or paced along the river bank at night,
Not silent, yet to such as passed them by
Quieter than lovers who have failed with kisses,
And so move, hand-divided to the world,
Yet secretly still interlocked with bliss.
Such grief was never known before, they said;
And watched him at a distance, day and night;
Solicitous to touch him, as though touch
Could break that concentration of despair
And call him back to life.   But they dared not.

The fourth day broke upon this hungry man
With stealthy light, and seemed to stoop above him
And wait there with that patience which we see
In those who bring release.   The watching brothers
Marked how he shuddered as the sunshine ran
Along the chapel pavement, in quick search
Of all suspended life, all winter grief.
They saw it flood about him, wake him up
From that long trance of mourning; draw him back
To this substantial world of earth and sun,
And things that grow, and flourish, and decay
In surety, strangers to the fantasy
Of human thought, and all its brood of shadows.

At last he rose, and swaying as he moved,
Crept out toward the daylight world of man.
But as he passed, the brothers saw his face,
And marked amid the ashen ruins of peace
A flame not seen there since the Abbot's ban
Had set the seal of contemplation
Before those eyes, and hid them from Earth's beauty.

They followed him with hushed tread from the chapel
Through the peach gardens to the river bank.
They saw him kneel there, lean above the brink
And gaze into the waters.   What he sought
None could conjecture; but he gazed so long,
They feared that grief had frozen up his mind.
But could that be? they asked each other.   Grief?
Could that quick flitting fire within his eyes
Be grief?   They looked again, and saw him staring
At sun-reflections in the shallow water,
And at the minnows darting through the weeds
Quicker than the penetrating light
Which followed them, and changed the bedded sand
To tiny ingots of bright river-gold.

Then they approached him, and he rose, and spoke.
'Brothers, I must go out into the world
And watch all things that move, and see the forms
Which changing life puts on, from birth to death.'
They could not understand.   What had these words
To do with that long vigil by the tomb?
They could not understand.   Even their love
Shrunk back from this divine irrelevance.
He walked downstream towards the open sea,
And they followed him no more, but took their way
Back to the cloister, musing as they went,
Until their wonder was dispersed in faith.

Craving for sleep, and satiate with hunger,
He reached the estuary, where the land
Was lost in reedy fens, which harboured none
Except the whining plover, and that faint
Far mockery of fire, the jack-o'-lantern.
His unacknowledged quest still urged him on,
Giving him certainty where there was none,
Giving him meat and wine although he starved.
And at the hour when early stars appear,
He left the marshes, found a fisher's cottage,
Knocked there, and took shelter for the night.

That eager mood protected him in sleep,
And warded off the nightmare forms of conscience.
He woke with guilt delicious on his tongue,
And the sharp fever of rebellion still
Fierce in his veins, and giving every sense
That swifter acumen such as we know
In moments of creation.

He arose,
And having eaten, left the gloomy hut.
Ah!   What awaited him!   The morning ripples
Ran with their little laughter up the beach,
And then with miniature pleasure broke
Scattering down the shingle in a white
Ecstasy of mingled foam and mist
That touched the invisible but ardent light
And chilled it into rainbows, cold as kisses
In the winterspring of youth.

                              He stood and watched,
Drinking the sight with sunken, greedy eyes,
That looked, and yet seemed half afraid to look,
Shrinking with shyness from this vision of joy,
Knowing themselves intruders from a world
Of heavier mould, and sun-excluding air.

He saw the seagulls dip to their reflections
In the sea-logged sand, as though they strove to feed
Those shadowy figures, touching beak to beak.
He saw the guillemot with clumsy flight
Encircled mockingly by crowding gulls,
Whose humour flashed broad-pinioned in the sun.
Along the dunes, where grow those sallow grasses,
Those cousins of the trailing ocean weeds,
He saw the cony sitting, and the quick
Strutting wagtail prying in the sand.
Then far out, lifted in the morning clouds,
Some lonely sails were lying, calm as thought,
And still as contemplation in the mind
Of one who wakes from sleep, to sleep again.

He stored these things up, and he went his way.
Treasure was in his path; but on he strode,
His greed increasing as he grew more rich
With this accumulation of delight.
He turned to the intense and brooding life
Of inland scenes, by which the ocean rhythms
Seem but the nursery songs of an earlier earth.
He watched the stately elm trees in the sun
Wrapped in their gently moving robes of light,
And visited by songsters, who would come
With momentary clamour, leaf and wing,

Then merge into the foliage, and be lost
One pausing instant—while the earth hushed and waited—
Then tune a note, then burst into a ripple
Of laughing song, and triple-sound the joy.

These things contented him, and fed his heart.
The shapely hills, the cottages of men;
The children, each a universe of hope;
The maidens, and the women big with child;
All these he saw, all Earth's propitiation
Of that insatiable desire within
Which urges her to make, and devastate,
And make again, until, her passion failing,
She joins at last those cold and lightless ghosts
That wander derelict among the stars.

And then his hand, subject so many years
To the soul's tyranny—that dared not grant
Even a partial freedom—now made claims
That would not be resisted.   He returned
To memories of a heron flying low
Over the cress beds by the abbey lakes.
He saw the evening sunlight on her wings,
And the low hills behind her, roseate
And filmed with dew-mists.   Framed about the scene
He saw the portal, underneath whose shade
A figure knelt, with scouring-stone in hand,
Drawing upon the flags his tribute to Earth
And all her flying beauty, and her moods.

But there was no rebellion now.   The pain,
The conflict, and the breaking down of bars,
The laceration as the fetters burst
Beneath that four-day tension of the spirit—
These agonies were over with the tumult
Which raged amid that vigil by the tomb,
When brethren stood afar off, cold with fear
Of the unnatural quiet where he knelt.

Many days above the truant's head
Passed with their gifts of shape, and hue, and motion.
He set these things down with a clumsy skill
Half reminiscent of the early years
Before dark conscience, jealous of a rival,
Put down the pride of craftsmanship, the joy
In nature, and sweet vanities of God.

Hour by hour, through those long summer days,
With never-flagging hand he strove to bring
The old skill back again, long forfeited.
All he remembered of those years was this,
The Abbot's warning, 'Is it blasphemy,
I wonder, to deny their strength and skill,
And starve them of their fitting avocation,
The praise, by imitation, of God's craft?'

But oh, how shy of him the world became!
Beauty seemed conscious of those clumsy hands,
And fled like Daphne, or became like her,
Changed in captivity.   Again he strove,
And yet again, a wisp of chill misgiving
Threading its way between the eager hours.
For Nature was resentful of neglect,
And went her way indifferent to his wooing.
Slowly, but with insistent power, the thought
Of failure rose, and turned his mind again
To the long-fostered habit of the cloister,
The inward brooding and neglect of joy.
The sunlight faded from the lapsing waves;
The sands no longer mirrored the blue sky
Nor lured the gulls with playful counterfeit
Of stretching wing, and grey flight-ruffled breast.

He felt the bitterness of failure creep
From vein to vein, like fever's antidote,
Quelling illusion and the sense of power.
But even this acrid medicine to his soul
Could not allay the long suppressed desire,
And he cried out upon himself: 'O fool!
What should you have to do with things of joy,
Earth's innocence, and folic in the sun?
They should be pictured by a lighter hand
That is not stiffened with a life of penance,
Nor robbed of skill by resolute denial.
Go you, therefore, and seek a fitter subject.
Are there not tears to find, and beauty smirched?'

And then he turned from Earth's inhuman candour;
Shunned all the interplay of light and colour
On wave and wing, on cloud and flower petal.
Some days he wandered effortless, outcast
From hope of Heaven and of new-found Earth.

Both seemed, since they had failed him, worthless gifts.
But in that semblance he perceived the lie,
And knew, although he dared not know, his loss.

Thereafter he sought out the wounded things,
Which earth shows in abundance, as though joy
And eagerness, and fierce creative pride,
Were but those fevers which the battlefield
Stirs in the hearts of all her living creatures.
So when the midday passion dies away,
There is the agony, the creeping home,
Broken, effortless—then the lonely death.

He painted children whom the grip of hunger
Had twisted, and made sullen.   But he failed.
The penetrating misery that sunk
Into their bones, and fouled the springs of childhood,
He could not capture that, and set it down.
He watched the peasant women in the fields
Toiling with men, though still their eyes were wild
With lingering pangs of childbirth.   Others he saw
Crippled with age and damp, and lifelong loss;
Weighted with bitter memories of loss,
Brooding above the stubble, robbed of hope
By the bare friendlessness of life with men;
Yet still within their hearts the embers of love,
That needed but a warm breath to revive
And burn again with a maternal light.
He tried to catch that pain, that fire, but failed.

He saw the young men stricken with disease,
With wounds, with vice, with lethargy of soul,
War's aftergifts, when all the murder is done,
And all the plunder gathered by the few.
He followed that corruption, face by face,
Eager to master every changing trick
By which it spoils the dignity of man.
He painted these, and looked upon his work
To see the passion there.   But he had failed.

With dogged purpose still he took the road,
Joyless and ungrieving, his spirit sleeping,
Numbed by the cheat of life.   Above his head
The intercourse of summer nights and days,

The timid lust, the lavish reticence,
Brought forth with teeming fruitfulness, the true
And ever-changing beauty of the earth.
But he was bowed low, and he could not see.

He trod the road, and came upon a hill
That rose toward a wooded crest, which stood
Bold in the light.   The trees with lifted arms
As though they greeted from their vantage-place
Some passing traveller from another world,
Reared up, and took the morning on their boughs
Shining with autumn fire.
                                        He raised his eyes,
Stirred for a moment, with a wakened pulse,
To fresh desire.   But then the inward canker
Ruined the illusion, and his eyes
Drooped again, and would have left him empty—
But in their fall, scanning the nearer ground,
They saw a human figure by the road,
Lying half buried in the seeded grass.

He stopped, and gazed upon the huddled shape;
Then spoke, gently, seeing that nothing moved.
It did not answer him, except to shrink
Closer about itself, as though it held
The very air suspect of cruelty
And merciless oppression.   He spoke again.
Then slowly from the poor convulsive frame
A moan escaped.   The effort of that pain
Racked every limb, and so revealed a man.
There was the ruin of beauty in his face;
A crumbled pride, and that fine wilfulness
Achilles wore when sulking in his tent.
But these were almost gone; and all the rest
Was gone, vanished with one consummate loss.
The empty sockets turned upon the monk
Cried out upon the evil work of man,
Venom implacable, and conscious hate.
Again the monk bowed down, for he had seen.

Then that same fever of the heron-flight
Possessed him, and he took with trembling hand
His crayons and his paper, and began.

Slowly the little flames of triumph crept
Into his brain, and set his mind on fire.
The very nerves along his fingers ran
With news of victory, and in his ears
Such exultation throbbed, beat after beat,
That the whole world was silenced round about him.
He did not hear the rustle of the grass;
The whispering leaves, the yellowhammer's song
Foretelling heat.   He did not hear the lark
Pouring her innocent delight abroad.
He did not hear the black lips cry for water,
And moan with unintelligible sounds,
Then cry again for water.
                              Slow time passed;
And the uplifted splendour of low light
Rose above the ridge, and left those trees
To a more sober noon.   Then evening fell;
And in the air, above the dying man,
A gnat-swarm hovered, veering in the sun,
A living shroud of such a gentle gold
As queens might envy.
                              Still the crayon moved,
Nearing achievement.   The hand which had impelled it
Faltered a little as the end approached,
Wearying toward the end, as all things do,
When in the effort of creative action,
Need for the final stroke drawing near, they pause
To brace themselves, and make the full conclusion.

So paused the monk: and all his senses dropped
Back into life a moment, while he breathed
A normal air, and rested from his labour.
He saw his work then as another would;
And saw that it was good.   The reassurance
Set the blood throbbing to his heart again,
Impatient to attack.   But, ere beginning,
He heard the murmur of those dying lips
Sink to a coherent cry for help.
'Fetch me a priest,' they said.   'Fetch me a priest.
Keep those faces from me: murdered faces!'
The crayon moved again; the voice went on,
Sinking slowly to the tone of death:
'Oh, treacherous!   That was an evil day.
Why do you come back?   Where is the priest?'

The priest bent to his task again.   The world
Was shut outside that inward tower of triumph.
The voice was shut outside, crying alone
In its remorseful wilderness.   The portrait
Of that cold lampless face became inspired
With the genius of darkness.   Those void sockets
Carried the scars of many an ancient wrong.
Our human tragedy lay in that face;
Fair promise; darkening noon; premature night.
There was the masterpiece, living for ever.
The voice was silent now.   The gnat-swarm still
Hovered above the unshrived man, its gold
Vanished with sunset, leaving but a grey
And ghostly shroud to sink upon the dead.

The dead?   The sea of inspiration ebbed.
The tower of triumph, now but a thing of sand,
Crumbled down, and left the tranced monk
Open to the onslaught of his senses.
His ears repeated to his waking brain
The dead man's cry, 'Fetch me a priest . . . a priest.'
He bent above the corpse, and listened close.
He heard that dark entreaty still.   It crept
From the cold lips of death, and filled the twilight
With omen; and the stars came, one by one,
Pronouncing judgment.   Night fell upon Earth,
And all her sounds, the nightjar, and the owl;
The rustling of the blindworm, creeping out
As silent as remorse.
                              The monk kept watch
Until the moon rose.   Then he bowed himself,
And froze the dead lips with an icy kiss.
They seemed to feel this Judas at the gate,
And shuddered, then to their unhallowed death
Returned.   Twice again he stooped and kissed,
Still without reason; cold, cold at heart.

Then, with the staring eyes of heaven above him,
Still without word or cry, he turned about,
Stretched forth his hands, and took in each a stone.
He seemed to pray a moment, as for strength;
Then rising, turned his face up to the sky,
And so put out his sight.
                              The cloistral walls
Encompassed him again, and now for ever.

When the day dawned, a shepherd found him kneeling
In prayer before the dead.   The shepherd knelt
Beside him for a while, then raised him up
And led him to the monastery, and told
A faltering story, how that he discovered
The blind priest watching by the side of death.
He gave them, too, the picture he had found,
And when they looked, they saw it was the face
Of their sad, holy brother, long familiar,
But now most strange, lacking the brooding eyes.
So they received their new elected Abbot,
And hung his portrait on their eyeless walls.

PHILIP

1920

My son, behold me here in Antioch,
Waiting the end.   And yet I may not murmur
Against fate or any cruel irony
Of slow-smiting time, the enemy of man.
For is not time a friend, bringing us peace,
Quelling alike our heart-beats and our pain,
Diminishing our personal tragedies
Until the distance swallows them?

                              My son,
Forbear a little from your enterprise,
Stay youth's desire a moment, while I speak.
I have this much of hopefulness concealed
In the last untouched corners of my heart,
This much, that when I see youth hot for action
And climbing boldly to the heights of thought,
I would cry out from dark experience,
Offering my guidance.   'Twill be scorned, I know!

But I have greater privilege to speak:
For in my youth I have had one adventure
Which shall be envied of the unborn world.
I sat with Christ at supper.   From that day
I have been far from human shores, my boat
Has tossed on rough seas, never charted yet,
And made discoveries that I would tell,
Knowing the world loves light despite its blindness.

To-night's the anniversary, the Passover,
A fitting time to tell you.   You have heard
Of Christ, the untutored carpenter, who came
From northern provinces to Jerusalem.
Strange, is it not, how his name and fame persist?

254

I chuckle now to think of all the hatred
That hissed about him.   He was like a star
Falling white-hot from the mystery of night
Into the Dead Sea waters!   What a smother!
What stinking steam arose.   The waters still
Bubble and froth, I am told; I am too far
To hear them now.   You have been taught in school
By the visiting priests, that boys should take as warning
This man and his rebellious works.   You were told
How early disobedience marked him, when he broke
The fifth Commandment—sacred to us Jews—
While still a boy: how he stole into the Temple,
Impudently discoursed with the sage elders,
What time his weeping parents searched in vain.
So from this sin, they teach you, he went on
To deeper infamies: forsook his trade
And family, and wandered labourless,
Trusting his wits to win him unearned bread.
That was a cardinal sin, counted to breed
Dissatisfaction in the labourer
And break his bondage of obedience
To Caiaphas and Herod, Church and State.
But there is more, this ne'er-do-well attracted
Dubious women about him, lived with one,
Nay, boasted himself the harlot's friend, and sat
Receiving sensual adulation from them,
Submitting to loathsome rites, in company
With publicans and sinners.   Still he sank
To lower depths, blaspheming the High God
From whom the priests held office; said the laws
Of Moses, the foundations of our State,
Were but a mortal code, and made to break
And amend.   Then went he to the Temple courtyard,
Where, by licence of the Church, the dove-sellers
Induce the people to make peace with God.
There like a madman he belaboured them,
Hoping in the ensuing confusion, to steal
Their money earned in holy service.   So,
Inevitable, the end came.   The people
Moved by a common impulse, national pride,
Outraged virtue, called on the priests for judgment.
The criminal was crucified; the warning
Hung in the archives of our righteousness.
Children, obey your parents, pay the priests
Fruit of your labour!

                              Thus to the end of time.
There may be priests one day who will enthrone
Christ as their God, and make his name a symbol
Of the dark powers of greed and temporal pride.
He, the simple lover of mankind,
May yet be used as the proud instrument
Of civilized oppression, truth's enemy.

Come closer, boy; my eyes are weak enough,
And the Spring daylight fails.   This freshening air
That creeps in from the sun-set like a breath
Of colour and blossom, is full of memories.
Thus touch and scent are agents of our souls.
Souls, do I say?   The term will serve us now;
Life's little definitions do not matter.
On such an eve as this it was, without
The city, dusk gathering under the green
Of the awakened trees, falling around pools
Whose deeps yet held a gleam of western light.
After the day's silence, a gentle swell
Of the foliage, a chill of the heart,
Joyful presage, anxious hope; while slowly
The land-air passed away to sea.   Earth moved
Uneasily, as though the Universe
Had made her centre of all scrutiny,
Expectant of that deed of deeds, forefelt
Since first creation sprang, which instantly
Revealed, shall tear the veil hanging 'twixt flesh
And spirit, and show the common parentage
Of sound and silence.   Such sweet promises
Life offers in abundance; they are the strength
Of beauty, and the lure of all our learning.
Still beauty promises, and still I learn,
Though stooping o'er the grave.   Is it with you
The same?   So shall it be with your son too,
So was it on the mountain-top, when Moses
Gazed towards Canaan, ere, as legend tells,
God took him unto rest.   I must believe
In that vast field of life beyond our flesh,
Inspired by such an immortality
Of promises.   This flesh is accidental;
But the dream that lingers in my mind has been
Hovering with vital influence over man
Immemorially.   Weigh the two, and feel
Earth's treasures trickle out between your fingers.

Such have I found it.   Christ was right in that.
I, holding all philosophy in my hands,
Have taken long to learn it: he was taught
Ah, who knows how?   He had a pretty symbol
For all this occult wisdom, saying, 'My Father,
He doeth the works!'   And still I say again,
'Show us the Father,' and shall, unto the end.

Hark you again, I have a word to say
Of that same criminal they crucified.
Best close the shutters; so we did that night,
Putting the world away, it seemed.   Now stir
The floating wicks, re-kindling for my eyes
Those little flames, which, born that night, are now
Clear altar-lamps to many worshippers,
Jets of a moment held imperishable,
Fixed for a beacon of eternity.
Such is man's power, to endow with lasting life
Things that were born for death.   This human passion
That can light up the universe, and hold
The fading stars in an undying legend,
Where shall its powers end, whence comes its strength?
I am perplexed—Christ answers it for me,
'Knowest thou not that I am in the Father,
And the Father in me?'—And still I am perplexed.
What do the Grecians call it?   Unscathed by names,
Upward it soars.   Perhaps on other stars
Circling the heavens about us, it is potent,
Flaming in souls half human, half divine,
Parent of hope, still nameless, reaching out
Beyond the grasp of us poor vessels shaped
To hold its primal kindling.

                                    Let me return.
These questions that tormented me that night,
Meriting Christ's rebuke, torment me still.

So came we to the city, chill and cold,
Wrapped in our mantles, pacing solemnly,
All of us heavy in thought, save only Peter,
He, the unquenchable talker, talking still,
But gloomily, as though the gathering night
Oppressed even him with beauty, and appalled
His garrulous tongue.   Judas Iscariot
Walked by my side, chinking the money-bag,
Fretfully sighing, till I was forced to whisper,

'What ails you, friend?'   Whereat, in undertones,
And stooping as he walked, he told me fear
Assailed him, for the Master's waste
Squandered our means; he would not let him save,
Nor would he preach again in Jerusalem
In the obscure quarters, drawing the fashionable world
Thereby, and filling up our common purse.
The Master walked in silence, at his side
Thomas and John.   The breeze athwart our path
Caressed John's reverent head, fluttered his beard
And mingled with his sighs, for he was sad.
Yea, were we all sad, entering the city,
Past the suspicious guard before the gates.
Heavily came we to the door of the inn,
Where two of our number awaited us.
                                        The Master—
—Mark you how I speak of him?   The memory
Of that one hour revives all reverence
That time and thought have striven to dissipate.
So deeply is it scarred upon my heart
That the chill floods of my maturer mind
Cannot remove it.   I am young again
Bathed in this tide of recollection; the years
Of slow advance to a more general wisdom
Submerge, doubts and life's-threshold visions revive.
Romance rekindles the nebulous void of life,
Then, still to be lived—now, lived and brought to ashes.

Peter went first; the Master followed him.
Slowly into the upper room we came,
He in the midst of twelve.   Quietness.   Peace.
Almost was audible the battling light,
The combat of the moon's ray with the flame
Of Roman lamps that made the chamber's gloom
Funereal.   Iscariot caught the light
Of the moonbeam, and sat in radiance,
I by his side in darkness.   My heart was dark,
Troubled with anguish, deep unrest and doubt.
Shame swept the arid desert of my mind.
I was a critic there, hated myself
Because loud Peter's mad infatuation
Moved me to scorn; hated myself again
For the incredulous wonder in my heart
When I beheld how John with passionate eye,
Love's soul, yearned at the man he knew was God.

Even now, half balanced on the edge of the grave,
Doubt—doubt—eternal doubt assails me.
This is life's tragedy, to lack assurance,
Never to find abiding place, where the soul
May sleep awhile, unguarded, confident
Of imperishable divinity,
Lulled by faith.   And yet—it smacks of the priests,
A comfortable creed, a fireside life.
I would not lose the biting recollection
Of windswept places, and the loneliness
Surrounding me in lands unpioneered,
Regions of stabbing darkness, where a man
Comes face to face with horror, the abysm.
Adventure of the spirit, denied to none
Who have the courage for truth!   Doubt is the air
Life breathes, the very atmosphere of health,
Stirring the heart to valour, and the soul
To passionate zest.   Well worth is all the pain;
I would not lose it for a peaceful death.
As I lived, so shall I die, in solitude,
Still journeying, my hunger unassuaged!

Thus sat we then at supper.   From below
Rose the low sound of human traffic over
The threshold of the inn, made sharp by night,
Yet dulled by the drawn curtains.   Once, a gust
Leapt in, as though the watching host of night
Prowled angrily without, with patient venom
Keeping an eyeless vigil on its prey,
Leashed, yet straining to unwary moments
Of leaping and caressing hate.   A lamp
Above the head of Thomas flickered out
Even as he spoke, his words thereby made darker,
'Lord, we know not whither Thou goest, and how
Can we know the way?'   Iscariot
Stooped from the moonray into darkness, peered
Slantwise into the Master's face, who sat
With trance-like vision gazing at the light
That glowed in the red heart of the wine flagon.
The words of his mouth, falling so gently down,
Burned me like fire, alighting on my ears
With a persuasion irresistible.
Fiercely I struggled in the outer dark
Against this blinding light.   As flame by flame,
So word by word descended, unhurried stream,

259

Yet pouring on my over-deluged ears
With cruel insistence.   My prison-breaking heart
Cried out, 'Let me believe; his works are good,
He is the soul of love; all charity;
All fierce denunciation of greed, of flesh,
Of sordid appetite, of all that mars
Each human day, and blots the resolutions
Of life's bright morn, conceived in innocence.'
And yet, from the dim recesses of my soul
A stranger voice, but more familiar,
Urged me, 'Beware, beware, it is not yours
To give this heart; you do not know yourself.
You are the present consummation of powers
Fled to the past where none may grope; the future
Hangs on your inward breathing, and is swayed
By an eyebrow's lift; this conscious heart and hand
Are but a moment's blossom; the root of you
Clings in the darkness with unrelaxing grip.'
And still his love assailed me, flame by flame,
And in new guise of proud humility
My heart, my very body, cried 'Surrender!
This shape you cling to, this deep inmost self,
Is but a shadow cast from his fierce light
Flickering with false, persuasive shapes, half born
Of outer chaos, half of your blind eyes!'
And still the remote voice from time's beginning,
'Flickers the shadow?   Then the flame veers too;
Beware! Beware!'   And I dare not believe,
Knowing the eternity of life, and the short span
Of our mortality.   Deep in my being,
Unknown then, now by labour made apparent,
Lurked the unchanging truth, that man's desire
Never shall circumscribe the force of life
Or harness with name and symbolic shape
The elusive all-pervading fire that lit
The singer David's heart, and forged in flame
Plato, the western dreamer whom I love.

Still the calm voice reigned level o'er the night,
'I am the way, the truth, and the life.   No man
Cometh unto the Father but by me!'
'Truth, truth,' re-echoed in my heart,
'Beloved, I behold in you my dream
Of man perfected, conqueror of fate!'

And, beating on my heart's constrained chambers,
'A symbol; 'tis but a symbol of the truth,
Your Self will serve as well.   Dream on a cloud,
A waterdrop, a stone; plumb to their depths—
There is revealed the Father!   Who is this
Dares to assume the rich prerogative
Of commonest clay?'   Foul fogs of black suspicion
Swept over me, and gasping death, I cried,
Finding an outward voice amid the babble
Of inward tongues, 'Show us the Father, Lord,
And it sufficeth us!'

                    Oh, foolishness,
That I should trust to vulgar mortal speech;
With these bare words a bumpkin might have uttered
Dragging the exalted struggle down from heights
Where my soul fought with time and space for vision,
Cleaving the illimitable, and reeling, blind!
And yet the Master knew me, took my words
As the inexpressive coinage of hope;
Saw not the common jeerer of the crowd
Who might have uttered them.   He looked within!
But baffling still the answer came; the stream
Of his unconquerable conviction flowed
Pauseless above the little dam I threw;
Flowed on, and bore me struggling in the flood,
Gasping for life, and clinging to the faint
Will-o-the-wisp, that firefly revelation
Which hovered before me then, and poises now
Beyond this shuttered window, where the last
Western gleam fades round the evening star.

Relumed the lamp, and Thomas shone again,
The common scepticism of the street
Glinting, half effaced, behind his eyes.
And was I one with him?   Christ knew the truth,
I heard beneath his words, though to us both
He spoke alike.   One terrible blow he struck
With cruel kindness to my heart.   I shrank
Back to despair, gasping for natural breath,·
Leaned in my fear against the wall, and wept
Inwardly, as a man uprooted weeps.
These were the words he spoke, that brought defeat
Looming upon my wearied soul.   'Or else
Believe me for the very work's sake, Philip!'

A little sophistry to vindicate
His mighty dream of salving the sick world;
Was it not simple and well justified?
Who with a mind of stone could have withheld
The gift of heart and soul against conviction,
Thrown doubts, half-doubts, unexplained desires,
All in the common cause with one belief,
One evident good, one certain cause for faith,
And drowned the insistent inner self in floods
Of overwhelming pity?   Such I did,
But with a coward's hand—or was it an act
Of some divinity within myself
Desperately anchoring itself to truth?
In the midst of my surrender I left one
Poor waif of thought to wander fetterless
In the dim regions of myself, that virgin forest
Upon whose marge I've travelled since that day,
And where I now camp for the final sleep,
My closing eyes turned to the untrod depths.

Silence fell, a gloom of fate impending.
There was a brawl of gallic mercenaries
Below, like mountain wolves at strife.   Shrieks rose
From some poor woman, victim of their lust.
There intervened the Roman guard, and peace
Reigned o'er the inn, save for the sobbing woman.

Then in the midst of supper, Christ arose,
Took bowl and linen cloth, and washed our feet.
Closer drew fate about our hearts, and sorrow
Hung o'er the feeble lamp-flames like a cloud
Spawned in the marshes of the outer world
When daylight creeps with waking disillusion
From the grey squalor of dull morning skies.
No single grief of any tangible shape
Could sear the heart so.   We were lifted up
To the vast sum of pity.   Humble man,
His lowly origin, and the brave quest
'Gainst giant odds and foes insensitive ;
All this we saw personified in Christ,
Centred in his simple act.   None spoke
Till honest Peter blundered into words,
Impervious to the suggestions of the air
And the whispering nothingness which teaches us
Most that we know beyond poor reason's grasp.

Slowly the fetters forged about my heart;
The little spark, starborn in woodland spaces,
Dancing through Time's beginning and beyond
Wide Space, now faltered out and feigned extinction.

Christ spoke again, and I saw Judas stoop
Over the ground, as though his soul had dealt
Blows on his guilty head.   Alas for him,
Symbol of common flesh, the sordid form
Of this people, nay, all the general world,
Rulers and ruled, youth and age alike.
He was a friend of priests and pharisees,
Makers of temporal place and pride of fortune,
Flesh-calculators, lasting enemies
Of healthy change, soul-freedom, bondless love
And the eternal revolution of hope.
Judas I call the enemy of youth.
Like flew to like—he went to seek the priests,
Things destitute of all imagination,
Born to crawl along the highway ruts
And pick the perishing treasures flung behind
By mad youth, by the young gods, by those
Who leap the hedge and strive unto the sun,
Frenzied with meadow-perfume and chance light
Caught from the eyes of creatures of the wood
And dewy hearts of flowers.

                            Such was Christ!
I have seen him—bah—what have I not seen;
How he would linger after a hungry day
To watch a cat tending its peevish kittens.
I've seen him, sick in body, dead with sleep,
Sit with a whore who feared she'd caught disease
From her last casual lover; sit talking there
Nightlong, until her dreary wailing ceased
And she went off, heart-cleansed.   Another band
Of irresistible belief bound me to Christ.
Sufficient that he asked my aid; was I
Lover enough of Judas and his like
Now to deny the man I fought beside,
Because we differed only in the choice
Of symbols?   He was God, he said; and I
—What was I?—God too, it matters not,
Thought I; the Sphinx still smiles inscrutable.

Iscariot took the cup, and stood revealed,
Child of this world—nay, child of this world's husk;
And I ranked closer with the man I loved.
Slowly the child of unimagination
Rose from the supper, crept toward the wall
Bowed by the weight of broken aspirations
Which tumbled about his head, erections built
On temporal sands with mortal calculation.
Hushed were the gazing twelve, each of his brethren
Consumed with fear, lest in the next assault
He should be sucked back by the common day,
Brought to the old world again—still so familiar—
And this unreal dream, this blissful tension
Of the soul's best part, relaxed, the normal state
Of this our human life on earth, resume
Its sway, half hope and half—blinding corruption.
Guilt tainted the silence; even John
Lost the rapt look of joy, drooping his head
On an uneasy bosom.   Christ alone
Dreamed undisturbed, oblivious of the bonds
This treachery had bound upon our conscience,
Urging us all to stand, for pity's sake,
More steadfast by his side.

                              Blind to the wall
Groped Judas, feeling his way with shameful hands
Until he reached the portal, and the lifting
Curtains, which the troubled winds of the world
Moved from without, as though in writhing torment.
It seemed the eternal enemy was waiting,
For as the cringing fingers grasped the folds,
Fumbling a little for lack of eyes to aid them,
Lo, a seething host of the invisible
Night, leapt in—fled back in instant terror
Of the calm glory and the unflinching lamps.
Up rose the curtain with uneasy moan,
Swelled out to falling agony, and dropped
Like a dumb limb of death between our world
And that which prowled without.
                              Judas was gone!

Then Christ arose, and took the bread, and brake it.
John raised his head, scenting forgiveness
Of the past poisoned moment.   God-like heart,

Seer of dreams, the poet-soul of conscience,
Bearer of others' pain, nearest to Christ!
Even Peter bowed his head, and wept,
Dazzled with prescience.   Faintness took my eyes
At this swift rush of spiritual events.
Plunged down, now brought to high expectancy
By the compelling ecstasy of light
Which lit the Master's eyes, gleamed in his hands
As with deliberate fingers they broke up
The Jewish bread—now doubly sanctified.
I heard him speak afar off, I sunk deep
In dreadful abyss, he raised on heights sublime.
With the divine conviction which no man
Might dare to hold, still he kept the symbol
Unmoved before his eyes; godlike, content
To summon this chaotic universe
In the one shape, the one name!   Oh, it maddens me
That I am cursed with such imagination
As whispers ever in my homeless brain
'It cannot be, it cannot be.   Beware,
Lest in the armour of this satisfaction
You stifle vision.   In such stability
Is death.'   I quelled the inward storm, and listened.
'This is my body, which is given for you.
Do this—. . . in remembrance of me.'
None answered; but we dimly understood.
Upon the face of one alone there shone
The glory of shared knowledge, and the light
Of prophecy.   Deep in my soul there sank
The heavy anchor of this sacrament.
With a rejoicing heart John saw this seed
Laid in our mortal earth, to bear its fruit,
A harvest for the hungry generations
Yet in the future's womb, waiting dark birth
Until it pleased the cycle of slow Time
To bring them forth, and rear them on this bread
To an uncertain strength, and confidence
In an eternal safety.

                          I am near
To the last supper of life, and now I take
The sacramental bread of death in hand.
It satisfies me not.   Likewise the cup
Leaves me athirst upon the desert's face,
And I stand fainting at life's final gates.

But, *there*—what chance had reason; nay, and more,
That higher logic of the soul, that force
Incomprehensible, beyond control,
Urging imagination to unrest
And time-destroying onslaught through the fields
Untroubled of mortality, where lurk
The constellations of unnumbered light
And Order has its primal seat?

                              I took
The bread, and drank the wine, as one entranced,
Dumbed with this poetry and high display
Of an appalling beauty.   Misty clouds
Veiled the far peaks of truth, breaking the light
Of human tenderness to rainbow glories,
Gracing deception with the form of hope.

My son, though life is not a thing of dreams,
Yet to the very end we grope our way
Half drugged with the strange poison of our blood.
All serves the same deceit; courage, desire,
Poor timid reason, love, the glorious birth
And dying beauty of all terrestrial shapes:
These breed despair and keep our eyes from vision.
Merged in the outer nothingness of death,
There shall I find perchance the source of life
Riven of form or any sensual moment;
All music ever on the verge of song,
Colour yet unborn within the ray,
The promise that will never need fulfilment,
The timeless, spaceless core, before whom fall
Our vastly apprehended gods, our mystic
Rites of high communion, and our faiths;
Blossoms whose birth is predetermined failure,
Since birth means death, and beauty is decay.
Life, the inspiration, is none of these!
In them, of them, and yet apart; the source,
The hope, the aim, and the last influence!

So glows the grave, a portal of clear light!
It is well earned; I have striven in my day.
Each man finds truth in his own fashion.   Christ
Offers good guidance; take his hand, believe
On him, learn from his proffered book of life. . . .

But then . . . turn inward, leave the Comforter,
Face the insatiable storm alone, and find
Your soul where lies the universe, where God
—So call him, if you need—sits ever enthroned
With the large congress of eternity.

Death grasps my body! 'Tis nothing!—My son, strive on;
The search is life.   The blindness of my birth
Breaks to the solemn twilight gloom of death.
It is the verge of morning.

                    I see a band
Crossing the Kedron brook without the City.
Unto the sorrowful Mount they go, for sleep.
This time I cross resolved on wakefulness,
And in the deathless garden of the grave
To experience the final agony,
Sweat bloody drops—and stand with Christ again,
Equal with him, self-guided to the end!

My son, do thus!   Christ sought to save the world,
And still the world is ripe with all corruption,
Still with idolatry it snares the soul.
You sprang from life—by your own way return.

Open the shutters now; the feast is done.
The cup of our communion is emptied;
The bread is eaten.   Now is the fitting time
For travel.   Bid me, bid Christ, farewell . . . and go!

PART TEN

EARLY POEMS

1910—1926

After the Storm

AFTER the rain had ceased
We wandered out again.
The trees and ripening grain
With beauty were increased;
And the flowers, heavy and bent,
Dropped an immortal scent.

There was no sunshine yet
As we strolled along the lane,
Slow, with a sweet regret
That still must cherish pain
Of angry word and look.
The boughs of love still shook
Keen drops about us there,
As closer still than ever,
We breathed the silver air,
Chill aftermath, but pure,
A passion to endure,
A love no storm could sever.

The Rebuff

The roses scratching at the window-pane
Whispered the scholar from his book, and stirred
Such trouble in him that the printed word
Was no more than a printed word again
Where lately it had touched him with the pain
Of princes who have learned from power. He heard
Such ghosts in that chance sound, that soon the blurred
And dimming page was wet with his heart's rain.

Fully a moment the intruder stood
Close on the threshold of his frozen mind,
But none may know that shape, nor what it sent
Burning from the past into his blood,
For though the roses still obeyed the wind,
Over his book, more resolute, he bent.

The Incentive

Drugged with happiness, they lived
Mute.   No agony of song
Told how well they thrived.
Unexpected grief ere long
Loomed upon the stream of days;
Sunshine colours cooled to greys,
Tear-clouds gathered, lightning flashes
Thrust, reducing joy to ashes.
After, when the storm had passed,
And a settled silence reigned;
From the lovers, torn and strained,
Music rose at last.

The Weapon

On a clear evening
When October closes
With wistfulness
Over the roses,
And the warm woodland
Changes to chill
Silver and silence,
The leaf-smoke rises
Against the dark hill
Acrid, spear-blue.

Even so, beloved,
Do I see you.

In the soul's autumn,
When hoar frost of thought
Has veiled the mind's blossom
With peace, gravely wrought
In silence and silver,
You rise from the mound,
The piled leaves of passion,
Like a spear from the ground!

Daybreak in a Garden

Weary with work
And daybreak vigil over words
I came down to the garden
And the deep linden grove.

O bosom of perfume,
Sustaining the anguished mind
With sleep-wisdom,
Draught of sensuous life,
And love without loss.

I lay along the level ray,
Lapped in light.
Sinking deep in the stream,
I found upon my right hand, sleep;
And on my left hand, dream.
From one to other swam
The pollen-dripping bees,
Heavy with honey-lime.
My thoughts were smeared and tangled in the scent,
And with their richness fell;
Fell into green profound,
Green deeper than knowledge
Or the religious sound
Of bread-breaking bell,
Bell of blood-sharing.
Down; no duty calling or caring;
Down; none to summon or tell;
Down into sleep I wound.

False Anchorage

Under this hayrick lies
All my heart's treasure.
The impermanent skies
Pass at their leisure,
And the flowers of the noon
Prepare to fade soon.
The bird-music dies.
Oh bitter heart's treasure,
To anchor me so
To this woman, my lover,
While the skies fade above her
And the earth dies below.

I

Smell the air
Everywhere!
What's the change?
Violet-range,
Primrose-track—
May's back!

II

Clover near the sedge grows,
Woodbine in the hedgerows
With the eglantine.
Poppy, pansy, marigold,
Blossoms rich and manifold . . .
All, all, all are mine!

III

Slippery chalk
On the downs
Hides away
Dainty gowns,
Primrose-yellows,
Bee-browns,
Violet.
Hail fellows . . .
Well met!

IV

Down, down,
Dirty drone;
Out of the hive!
Fat, blown,
Overgrown,
No one to wive.
Queen's wed,
Drones are dead. . . .
Now we can thrive!

V

Sun sets,
Petals close,
Honeybag's swollen.

Home gets
Bumble-nose
With nectar and pollen
From pistil and stamen,
Half alive,
She seeks the hive,
Buzzing her
Amen.

VI

Safely home, home at last,
All the travel done;
All the weary hours are passed,
All the daylight's gone.

VII

Ah, the honey of desire,
Hearth and home and fire
In the hive of our delight
Eager music through the night;
Vibrant love when all is still,
Cold, and dark upon the hill
Where the blossoms sleep that fed
The golden glory of our bed,
The Queen, the Queen of Honeycomb
Reigning o'er her regions vast. . . .
Safely home.
Home at last!

Star-worship

I see the brightest star of heaven to-night.
Ah, beautiful, I come to you, I come
Loud with the silence of delight
And unborn music dumb.

How I recall the worship of my youth,
The striving after space, star beyond star!
But now I find a wider field of truth
Where'er my fellow men and women are.
The god behind the stars I find
Less mysterious than my mind;
And no more in a comet's flash
Than in a burnt stick's ash.

A Wild Night

The ivy beats upon the wall,
The owls across the blind fields call,
And the oak by the housedoor
Bends stiffly down, to implore
Mercy, mercy of the wind.
But other hordes race up behind,
And his aged limbs are twisted and tossed,
And the skies are stung with the twigs he's lost,
While he groans by the housedoor.
The carpets swell above the floor,
And the fireside cat, coiled up for sleep,
Feels her fur rise, her flesh creep.
Closed doors rattle at their locks;
And the crowing of the midnight cocks
Is caught and tossed from side to side
Of the shrunken sky as the winds ride
Shrieking aloud, booming with deep blast,
Whispering—hissing with lips aghast,
Blowing on, on with bateless strength
Till the gentle elms are laid full-length,
And the larch is shaken and falls in the wood,
And leans in the arms of those that have stood
Around it, its brothers, from birth till now,
This moment of groaning root and torn bough.
The dark aisles of the wood are strown
With dead limbs, longtime grown
Sapless and brittle, that once blew
Limeflower secrets the summer through,
Now splintered, pulled from their lichened sleep
By these hordes that pounce and leap
With shrill cry, with deep roar, with faint
Whisper, distant sighings, and that restraint
Which preludes invulnerable onslaught
And fiercer combats to be fought.
—Now the wind slacks—the trees arise
And, cold with terror, scan the skies
To learn if it's over, the agony done,
. . . But no! new assaults have begun!

The Tide

The heavy burden of the sun
Fell from the stooping day.
A sighing air was felt to run
From seaward over the bay.

Then in the shallow waters and the pools,
Sand-rippled treasuries of fallen tides,
And rocky clefts full vision-deep,
To whose calm wells the eyeshaft glides
Wonderingly, while expectation cools
To merman greetings, and cold sleep
Under blunt-fingered weeds,
A little movement of the sea
Came in to greet them, to wake their lethargy,
Stirring them from isolated dreams
With new, insistent, inter-running streams,
That crept around the ridges of the sand,
Making innumerable partings, innumerable joins,
Until they lapped the bases of the groynes.
Sandworm spirals, near an inch in height,
Slowly dissolved, and little shells, dry on land,
Were neared, and touched, and tipped,
Then quietly, suddenly into the water dipped,
And rebaptized with colour and cold flame,
Such as the nereids in their bosoms frame,
Laying between their pearly breasts at night
Mortal enchantments, but seagods' delight.

Slowly the sandy wastes, the dark and dank
Heaps of the drifted weeds, sank . . . sank,
Kissed once again with the light-enamoured lips
Of the wavelets running with laughter and ripple of spray
Into the shallows and hollows and folds of the bay,
Clean as the mirth at the bows of deepsea ships.
Then rank on rank the foremost waves swept in,
Arches of beauty, moulded with light therein,
Western colours, on their backs the rainbow ray,
Creatures born of midocean and robed in the fall of day.
And now, where the curves of the beach were lifeless and dull,
Is water, dancing and deep, swinging and clear,
Wilful and changeful, swift as the wing of the gull;
While the deep-toned songs of the oceanides draw near.

The Lantern

She swings the lantern.   Night around her
Swings out, swings in; the roadside falls.
Under her feet abysmal darkness sinks;
Then from the pit, to meet her feet,
Earth rises, sombre stones and steady soil
Loom up, stare at the lantern, then . . .
Sink, sink again as it swings.

On she tramps, towering above the lantern,
All her daylight beauty lifted away,
Underlit, and drenched with the dye,
The smudgy gold of the drowsy beams from the lantern.
Over the light her hip turns smooth and strong,
Rolling the shadows to and fro on its breadth,
To and fro in rhythm as on she swings.—
The gaunt trees over her leap, and mope, and bow.—
And one deep breast, like the old moon lacking light,
Rides above, rimmed with a ghostly line;
Then waxes full as the lantern swings before.
Crowning this wild-lit moving life,
The aureoled hair glows gold, a smoke-veiled fire,
Flaming and changing, but ever her crown as she swings
On, swings on, steady and sure, while the earth and skies
Tumble and leap and prance and dance round the lantern.

The cows are milked; she is going home to her babe.

The Mill Pond

Deep, deep beneath the surface of the mere
Lie the green lifting avenues of sleep.
There lurk the drowsy carp year after year.
Ever rising from the central deep,
Wells within placid waters, the dark springs
Cast circling forms that rise on watery wings,
Trouble the water-weeds, trouble the surface calm,
Smooth into stillness, as a warm-lifted palm
Lifts its green plumes along the desert air,
Moved by far-roaming breathings from the sea,
That pass, leaving deeper tranquillity.

Green are the margins of the mere.   Rustling there,
Bulrushes sway,
Chafing their velvet sceptres night and day,
Noiseless movements, swaying heads of brown,
Creating little ripples, that far, far down,
In timid worlds of glassy images,
Break shapes of brown, unweave the green,
Mingle the two, walling the avenue
With lifting hues of brown and greening glooms.
Out in the shelving central mere there looms
The crater of the rising waters.   There contend
Strange windless clouds, far, far below;
There from the bosom of the underworld
Dim constellations gleam, vanish, and glow
As wandering airs disturb their haunts, and wend
Slowly away, leaving the night unfurled
Far, far below, reflected again, as death
Refills the mirror after life's last breath.

Evening

Only an old woman going home under the pines,
And the sough of the wind before her and the sigh of the wind behind.
A petulant grumble stored up in the back of her mind
At the past that is gone before her and the death that she half divines
In the moan of the wind before her and the sob of the wind behind.
Only an old woman going home under the pines.

Interlude at the Dance

Cloaking her round, I took her from the dance,
Covering her beauty up, her golden head,
And those entrancing arms.   Gently I led
The virgin wonder forth, without a sound
Tiptoeing to the margin of the night,
Seeking adventure in the care of chance,
Chance, and that deep power which leads us on,
The destiny of hearts.

A bell boomed the hour,
Casting a flight of sound over the town;
And the loomed creeper swayed as the air passed
Heavy with bell-music.   Things so slight
Troubled us, touching deeper tones within,
So that we clung together in distress,
Joyful distress, such as that which wrung
The hearts of Tristan and Isolda once
At the ship's prow, sailing the dark seas.

Shivering in the cool air, she looked up,
And her pallid brow, and her bright dance-flushed cheeks,
Gleamed like a southern moth in the lantern glow.
And her trembling mouth too . . . As a child seeks
The mystery of the flowers, my mouth sought hers,
And we clung, oblivious of the chill night hours.
We took our fill of all the joys unsung,
And all the hidden splendour of young life.

Then, troubled with strife so unforeseen, so strange,
Throbbing with all the tumult that the earth could lend her,
She whispered unbidden, 'Take, take, and spare not.
It is no sin!' and I saw her soul range
Over the universe, asking what this might mean.
Then the response within me rose—'Take, take!'
But seeing her soul craving to be told,
I grew of a sudden chilled and old—and she,
Seeing me pause irresolute, knew that we dare not.

She arose, and we went in, silently.

The Ruined Cottage

Overrun with hemlock,
Over-arched by lime,
Lies the crumbling cottage,
Victim of old Time.

Through the flint wall passing,
Reach the open grate.
Here on winter evenings
Grandfathers sate.

Here they read their Bibles
Heard of war in Spain;
Rugged with their lifelong
Reaping of the grain.

Here the girls grew comely,
Laboured long and late,
Till hard wedlock took them
To another state.

Here the maiden longing,
Here the boyhood dream,
Girded at the harness
Of the master's team.

Up the breakneck staircase
Crept the wedded wife,
Lay and took the bitter
Full fruits of life.

This low raftered ceiling
Held her glazing eyes
When the pangs of childbirth
Spoiled love's paradise.

Down she crept, child-weary,
Still afraid to rest;
Laboured in the meadows,
Fever in her breast.

At last, with twisted body,
To the home she kept;
Watched with fear her daughters
Growing love-adept.

From this door her son went,
Lured by Glory's lie;
For nobody's quarrel
In strange lands to die.

Here the rheumatism
Gripped her man at last;
And the workhouse spectre
Loomed above them vast.

Underneath the lintel
Hunger found a way,
Hemlock in the garden
Strengthened day by day.

Gratitude of master
Passed the cottage by;
Winter followed winter,
Bared the roof to sky.

Grassmounds in the churchyard;
Obscure beds of sleep.
By the silent threshold
Graze the master's sheep.

Overrun with hemlock,
Over-arched with lime,
Lies the crumbling cottage,
Victim of old Time.

INDEX OF FIRST LINES